A FUNDER'S GUIDE *from*
Fieldstone Alliance & GEO

A Funder's Guide to Evaluation: Leveraging Evaluation to Improve Nonprofit Effectiveness is one of a series of works published by Fieldstone Alliance in collaboration with Grantmakers for Effective Organizations (GEO). Together, we hope to strengthen nonprofit organizations, the communities they serve, and the nonprofit sector by helping grantmakers in their work with nonprofits.

a Funder's Guide to

EVALUATION

Leveraging evaluation
to improve nonprofit effectiveness

Peter York

FIELDSTONE
ALLIANCE

SAINT PAUL,
MINNESOTA

We would like to thank The David and Lucile Packard
Foundation for support of this publications.

Fieldstone Alliance is committed to strengthening the performance of the nonprofit sector. Through the synergy of its consulting, training, publishing, and research and demonstration projects, Fieldstone Alliance provides solutions to issues facing the nonprofit sector. Fieldstone Alliance was formerly a department of the Amherst H. Wilder Foundation. If you would like more information about Fieldstone Alliance and our services, please contact Fieldstone Alliance, 60 Plato Boulevard East, Suite 150, Saint Paul, MN 55107, 651-556-4500

We hope you find this book useful! For information about other Fieldstone Alliance publications, please see the ordering on the last page or contact:

Fieldstone Alliance Publishing Center
60 Plato Boulevard East
Suite 150
Saint Paul, MN 55107
800-274-6024
www.fieldstonealliance.org

To learn more about the TCC Group, contact:

The TCC Group
50 East 42nd Street, 19th Floor
New York, NY 10017
212-949-0990
www.tccgrp.com

Edited by Vincent Hyman
Designed by Kirsten Nielsen
Cover Illustration by Brian Jensen

Manufactured in the United States of America

First Printing, June 2005

Library of Congress Cataloging-in-Publication Data

York, Peter, 1967-
    A funder's guide to evaluation : leveraging evaluation to improve nonprofit effectiveness / by Peter York.
        p. cm.
    Includes bibliographical references and index.
    ISBN-13: 978-0-940069-48-0 (pbk.)
    ISBN-10: 0-940069-48-2 (pbk.)
    1. Nonprofit organizations--Evaluation. 2. Evaluation research (Social action programs) I. Title.
    HD2769.15.Y67 2005
    658.048--dc22
                        2005010357

About the Author

PETER YORK is vice president and director of evaluation at TCC Group, a twenty-five-year-old firm with offices in New York, Philadelphia, and Chicago. He leads the firm's evaluation practice and serves on its board of directors.

TCC Group provides management consulting, strategic planning, and evaluation services to nonprofit organizations, private foundations, and corporate citizenship programs. The firm has assisted a variety of funders in designing and implementing evaluations using evaluative learning tools and strategies, including the David and Lucile Packard Foundation, James Irvine Foundation, William and Flora Hewlett Foundation, William Penn Foundation, Howard Hughes Medical Institute, Charles Stewart Mott Foundation, Ruth Mott Foundation, Community Foundation of Greater Flint, United Way of Genesee County, Massachusetts Cultural Council, New England Foundation for the Arts, Prudential Foundation, Sierra Health Foundation, Wachovia Foundation, and Pfizer Foundation.

Peter provides consulting services to nonprofits and grantmakers. He has published articles and conducted numerous workshops related to evaluation and capacity building. He also served as a project director for one of the first applications of using a "theory of change" approach to evaluating community initiatives; he coauthored a chapter in the book *New Approaches to Evaluating Community Initiatives—Volume 2: Theory, Measurement, and Analysis*, published by the Aspen Institute in 1995. He also spent seven years working in direct practice as a mental health and case management service provider prior to becoming a consultant. He conducted his graduate studies at Case Western Reserve University's Mandel School of Applied Social Sciences, where he earned his Master's Degree in Social Service Administration and is "all but dissertation" on his Ph.D. (ABD) in Social Welfare.

Peter York can be reached at TCC Group, One Penn Center, Suite 1550, Philadelphia, PA 19103, 215-568-0399 ext. 202, pyork@tccgrp.com.

Acknowledgments

I want to thank all the people who helped during the writing of this book by providing guidance and support, sharing their experience, and reviewing the manuscript:

Paul Connolly	John Riggan
Deborah Felix	Felipe Rivera
Mark Hertle	H. Mark Smith
Chantell Johnson	Steve Vetter
Christine Koehn	Kathleen Wagner
Steven LaFrance	Karen Walker
Richard Mittenthal	

I want to thank all of the nonprofit leaders, grantmakers, and researchers whose work I cite—the list is too long for individual names. They have made major contributions to the capacity-building and evaluation fields, including developing the models for understanding and improving evaluation use that were critical to the writing of this book.

I want to thank Lori Bartczak from Grantmakers for Effective Organizations for her patience and extremely helpful and thoughtful editorial support, and the Fieldstone Alliance staff—Vince Hyman and Kirsten Nielsen—for their time, attention, wisdom, patience, and guidance during book development.

I am especially thankful to my colleagues at TCC Group who contributed to the creation of this publication, including John Riggan, Richard Mittenthal, Paul Connolly (who worked with me to develop the organizational effectiveness model that was incorporated into this book, and provided significant substantive and professional advice and guidance throughout the process), Chantell Johnson (who provided content advice, significant input on the overall approach, as well as examples from her significant evaluation experience), and Cara Cipollone (for contributing to the development of the briefing paper that this book is based on). I also greatly appreciate all my clients, who imparted their wisdom to me over the years. Through sharing and by example, they helped me learn about how evaluation is viewed and works in the real world.

Lastly, I want to thank my wife, Maria, who by example reminds me that learning in life comes not in the form of the facts and figures that we gather along the way, but in the meaning that we make and the resulting actions that we take in the pursuit of improving the way we live. Thank you for your wisdom and support throughout this journey.

Contents

Chapter 4

Step-by-Step Strategies for Supporting the Use of Evaluation as a Capacity-Building Tool

Introduction

The Case for Using Evaluation as a Capacity-Building Tool

EVALUATION'S SOLE FUNCTION IS OFTEN ACCOUNTABILITY: nonprofits evaluate their programs to prove to funders that their programs are needed and effective, and funders conduct evaluations to prove to their boards, the field, and other key constituents that their grantmaking efforts are strategic and effective. However, accountability should seldom be the only role for evaluation.

More and more funders and nonprofit leaders are shifting away from proving something to someone else, and toward improving what they do so they can achieve their mission and share how they succeeded with others.

For example, the Philadelphia Zoo recently began designing a system to evaluate whether its guests and program participants are moving from a level of awareness about conservation issues toward taking conservation action in their lives. An objective of this system is to evaluate which program qualities lead to the greatest improvements in conservation behavior. The goals of the system are to assess the types of conservation behavior the Zoo is affecting, to understand how best to use the Zoo's resources, and to identify which types of guests will benefit most. The Zoo intends to use the system to better understand if and how it is achieving its mission, as well as to disseminate what it is learning to other zoos throughout the country. This is a sophisticated evaluation, designed from the start to help the Zoo learn to improve its mission impact.

More and more funders and nonprofit leaders are shifting away from proving something to someone else, and toward improving what they do so they can achieve their mission and share how they succeeded with others.

Examples such as this are encouraging, but generally the field needs a better understanding of how evaluation can serve as a learning or capacity-building tool.

For the purposes of this book, the use of evaluation as an organizational capacity-building tool will be referred to as *evaluative learning.* It is my hope that this term will lessen the negative connotation often associated with the term *evaluation,* and incorporate and emphasize the desired capacity-building outcome of learning, rather than describing an evaluation approach or process.

The idea of using evaluation for ongoing learning is not new. Many evaluation leaders in the field have developed and refined the use of evaluation as a learning tool. For example, Michael Quinn Patton is known for developing the "participatory evaluation" approach, which he defines as "a process controlled by the people in the program or community. It is something they undertake as a formal, reflective process for their own development and empowerment."[i] David Fetterman developed the "empowerment evaluation" approach, which is designed to "help people help themselves and improve their programs using a form of self-evaluation and reflection."[ii]

How to Use This Book

This book is designed to help funders decide whether and how to support the use of evaluation as an organizational capacity-building tool. This book is written to be a practical and user-friendly guide that provides the concepts and tools for funders to support their and their grantees' evaluative learning efforts.

The book is organized into four sections.

Chapter 1: Evaluative Learning: The Centerpiece of Capacity Building. This section presents a definition and description of capacity building, as well as a model of organizational effectiveness. It discusses how evaluation can and should serve as the key capacity-building tool that will lead to achieving organizational effectiveness. It presents a definition of evaluative learning, the approach that is offered in this book for using evaluation as a capacity-building tool.

Chapter 2: How Evaluative Learning Builds Capacity. This section presents an overview of how funders and nonprofit organizations typically use evaluation. The current state of the field serves as the jumping-off place for presenting a model of organizational learning, the cornerstone of which is evaluation. This section also includes a set of strategies for using evaluation as a capacity-building tool to improve organizational functions like strategic planning, human resource development, board development, and fundraising.

Chapter 3: Grantmaker and Grantee: Partners in Evaluative Learning. This section, the largest of the book, describes the philosophical change that many funders will need to make if they are to support their grantees' use of evaluation as a capacity-building tool.

Chapter 4: Step-by-Step Strategies for Supporting the Use of Evaluation as a Capacity-Building Tool. This section walks readers through a step-by-step process that funders can use to build the evaluative learning capacity of their grantees. The specific steps are as follows:

Step 1: Educate board and staff—helps board and staff understand the benefits, compromises, and challenges of supporting evaluation as a capacity-building tool.

Step 2: Assess organizational readiness—identifies critical factors that will determine a funder's readiness to shift current evaluation practices toward evaluative learning.

Step 3: Determine where to begin—helps funders assess their current grant portfolio to select a program or outcome focus area for supporting evaluative learning.

Step 4: Assess grantees' current efforts—provides funders with the information they need to discover grantees' current evaluation efforts and find out the evaluation requirements that other funders ask of them, with a goal toward aligning these activities.

Step 5: Identify a set of grantees to support—helps funders assess their grantees' readiness for evaluative learning and decide which organizations to invest in.

Step 6: Understand strategies for supporting evaluative learning—presents a number of low-cost to high-cost evaluative learning strategies that a funder can support.

Step 7: Set criteria, select strategies, and begin work—helps funders determine the amount of resources that both the funder and grantee have to invest in the effort, determine which particular strategy will garner the greatest capacity-building impact, and decide where to begin implementing evaluative learning approaches.

This book also provides several tools that will help funders decide if and how to support evaluation as a capacity-building tool, as well as determine the most cost-effective strategies for doing so.

- A tool for assessing funder readiness
- A simple logic model development tool
- A questionnaire for determining grantees' evaluation efforts and assessing their readiness for evaluative learning
- A tool for assessing the best evaluative learning support strategy, including estimates of associated costs

These tools are also available in electronic form online exclusively at the publisher's web site. Buyers of this book may download them at no cost. To access these tools, go to the following URL and follow the download instructions:

http://www.fieldstonealliance.org/worksheets1.html?069482

These materials are intended for use in the same way as photocopies, but they are in a form that allows you to type in your responses and reformat the material. Please do not download the material unless you or your organization has purchased this book.

Chapter One

Evaluative Learning: The Centerpiece of Capacity Building

P AUL CONNOLLY AND CAROL LUKAS DEFINE THE TERM capacity building as "the process of strengthening an organization in order to improve its performance and impact."[iii] Examples of capacity-building activities include strategic planning, board development, communications, upgrading technology, increasing fund development capability, planning and developing facilities, acquiring new equipment, acquiring new staff, improving staff knowledge and skills, and evaluating programs.

Typically, the types of capacity-building efforts nonprofits spend the most resources on are those most directly tied to programs and services, such as fundraising, human resource development, and general operations (including things like financial management, facilities planning, and management). These are the "nuts-and-bolts" capacities necessary for achieving an organization's mission.

Over the past five to ten years, nonprofits have begun to realize that nuts-and-bolts capacities are not enough to be effective. Clearly, leadership and planning are prerequisite organizational capacities required to ensure that all other organizational capacities, including programs and services, most effectively serve the mission. Through the educational efforts of the

Organizational planning and leadership decisions are often conducted without an ongoing and clear understanding of the quality and success of programs. A well-framed and well-designed evaluation, conducted regularly, increases the quality of organizational decision making.

management assistance field, including organizations like Grant-makers for Effective Organizations and the Alliance for Nonprofit Management, more and more nonprofits are taking steps to strengthen their planning and leadership efforts.

Program evaluation is another key capacity necessary to become a true learning organization. To date, many nonprofit leaders have viewed evaluation as a responsibility they must meet for their funders, but less so for their own organization, their clients, or the community. In 2001, a study of California nonprofits that found that only 13 percent of nonprofit leaders (who responded to a survey on their capacity-building efforts) consider evaluation a top priority with respect to their capacity-building efforts.[iv] As a result, organizational planning and leadership decisions are often conducted without an ongoing and clear understanding of the quality and success of programs. That's too bad; a well-framed and well-designed evaluation, conducted regularly, increases the quality of organizational decision making and decreases the likelihood that important information will be missing from organizational decision making.

Before putting forth a definition of "evaluation for capacity building" or "evaluative learning," it is important to understand the key capacities all nonprofits need to be effective. Understanding the big picture for how nonprofits function helps us understand the important role program evaluation plays in achieving organizational effectiveness. This chapter will discuss

- Core organizational capacities
- How evaluation can serve as a capacity-building tool
- What evaluative learning is

Core Organizational Capacities

In a recent study of management support organizations throughout the country, TCC Group put forth a model for understanding the core organizational capacities that nonprofits must have to be effective.[v] This model is not proposed as the only or best model, but rather as a framework for describing the capacity needs of the nonprofit sector. Central to this model is the identification of four core capacities nonprofits need to achieve their mission:

- Leadership capacity
- Adaptive capacity
- Management capacity
- Technical capacity

Leadership capacity: The ability of all organizational leaders to inspire, prioritize, make decisions, provide direction, and innovate to achieve the organization's mission. Effective leadership is really about seeing the next step the organization needs to take to achieve its mission—providing a clear set of goals and objectives and providing the direction and inspiration for carrying out a plan of action.

Adaptive capacity: The ability of a nonprofit organization to monitor, assess, respond to, and create internal and external changes.[vi] Many changes affect the health of a nonprofit. Internal changes include things like staff or board member turnover and changes in quality of programs or in organizational culture or structure. External changes can include things like new or reduced funding streams and changes in governmental policy or in the nature and scale of a problem within the community. Nonprofits need to be able to respond to all these changes if they are going to survive and thrive. However, responding to change is not enough. Nonprofits must also have the capacity to create changes inside their organization and in the community if they are to sustain their work and ultimately achieve their mission. Adaptive capacity is about an organization's ability to respond to changes it doesn't directly control, and to create changes to gain more control.

Management capacity: The ability of a nonprofit organization to ensure the effective and efficient use of organizational resources. Management capacity differs from leadership capacity in that leaders envision the future, set priorities, goals, and objectives, and make resource allocation decisions, while managers ensure that all resources (human, financial, technological, facilities, and so forth) are used in the most effective and efficient way to achieve the goals and objectives. (Note that any one individual within an organization can have both leadership and management roles.)

Technical capacity: The ability of a nonprofit organization to implement all of its key organizational and programmatic functions. The technical capacity of any organization is reflected in how it applies the knowledge, skills, and experience of its staff to implement all organizational tasks. For example, every organization needs individuals who know how to recruit donors, run software programs, deliver programs and services, or communicate effectively with community leaders. While there are common technical functions for all nonprofits, each organization also has a unique set of technical functions specific to the type of work it does and how its organization is operated.

Figure 1, Core Organization Capacities, presents how specific organizational functions, like fundraising, financial management, human resource management, and strategic planning, are reflected in these four core capacities.

Figure 1. Core Organization Capacities

Capacity	Function
Leadership capacity The ability of all organizational leaders to inspire, prioritize, make decisions, provide direction, and innovate to achieve the organization's mission	• Board/governance • Leadership development • Executive transition • Strategic planning (prioritizing and making decisions)
Adaptive capacity The ability of a nonprofit organization to monitor, assess, respond to, and create internal and external changes	• Client needs assessment • Program evaluation • Organizational assessment • Collaboration • Networking • Strategic alliances and restructuring • Strategic planning (reviewing and assessing all client, organizational, and programmatic information
Management capacity The ability of a nonprofit organization to ensure the effective and efficient use of organizational resources	• Human resource management and development • Financial management • Knowledge management • Facilities management
Technical capacity The ability of a nonprofit organization to implement all of its key organizational and programmatic functions	• Program or service delivery • Fundraising • Marketing • Technology • Accounting • Research (data collection and analysis) • Communication • Public relations • Outreach

How Evaluation Can Serve as a Capacity-Building Tool

Evaluation is a crosscutting capacity that can be used to improve all four capacities (leadership, adaptive, management, and technical) presented in Figure 1, Core Organization Capacities.

Evaluation to improve leadership

Nonprofit leaders, armed with better information about how well their programs are doing, can make better decisions about how best to use their limited resources. For example, imagine that a job-training organization learned through evaluation that program participants who received one-to-one coaching stayed in their job longer than participants who did not receive coaching. This information would help organizational leaders decide how to shift resources toward the coaching service; it would also support requests for additional funding for coaching.

Innovation could increase, too, as the organization's leaders learn to evaluate the effectiveness of new ideas. For example, if leaders of the same job-training program wanted to start an ongoing peer support program, their evaluation efforts could test this new effort to see if the peer support program increased the length of time participants remained in their job. If the evaluation found that this support group didn't make a difference, then leaders could make better use of the time and money they put toward this service.

Finally, leaders can also share successes with their staff as a way to inspire continued improvement. Nonprofit staff sometimes see evaluation as a burden, rather than as constructive. However, when leaders share with staff the strengths that evaluations have identified, evaluation motivates and inspires continued improvement.

Evaluation to improve adaptive capacity

Program evaluation is an adaptive capacity tool because it provides the information an organization needs to respond to organizational or environmental changes affecting the quality and effectiveness of its programs. Consider the example of the evaluation of a literacy program. Through study, evaluators found that the number of adult volunteers who read to kids had decreased by a third, and that a large percentage of the remaining pool of volunteers had decreased the frequency they volunteered from once a week to once every three weeks. With this information, the organization would have a clear indication of changes in its recruitment strategies (an internal problem) or in the lives of adults in the community (an external problem). As such, it could begin to develop informed strategies for addressing these potential internal or external problems.

Evaluation to improve management

With high-quality evaluation, nonprofit managers can better monitor, assess, and adjust organizational and programmatic resources. Let's say an organization that provides homeless people with access to job opportunities is evaluating the quality of the following services: identifying potential places of employment in the community, building relationships with the leaders of these local businesses, placing homeless persons in jobs at these businesses, and providing transportation and job coaching for six months after placement. Now, assume the evaluation found that many of the best placement opportunities still required workers to walk a considerable distance to get to the job. As a result, the evaluation showed that clients were often not showing up to work on days of extreme weather. With these evaluation findings, the program managers of the nonprofit organization would be in a better position to strategize about how to use existing resources more effectively or to identify additional resources to resolve the problem. For example, managers might try to make arrangements with the employers to pick up people at the bus or train stops on days of inclement weather.

Evaluation to improve technical capacity

Finally, evaluation provides nonprofits with information necessary to ensure that staff have the technical skills and knowledge to do their jobs well. Take the example of a program that pairs high school students with university research scientists. The goal is to increase student motivation to pursue careers in science. Key to this work is the scientist's ability to teach and mentor students while conducting research. Imagine that the evaluation assessed the quality of the scientist's interactions with the student. Through the evaluation, this program might discover that some students are not seeking out additional science courses or extracurricular activities, while others are doing so. If the evaluation focused on both this outcome and the quality of the interaction between the scientist and the student, evaluators might discover that the students who did not pursue additional science opportunities had spent their lab time with the scientist mentor cleaning lab equipment or running errands rather than receiving opportunities for one-on-one learning. Program managers could then develop strategies to build the scientists' technical capacity as teachers and mentors.

> **Evaluative learning is an ongoing, collaboratively designed, and stakeholder-led evaluation process that has the primary purpose of serving organizational learning by evaluating the whole logic model.**

As the examples cited above show, evaluation is a crosscutting capacity-building tool that, when used appropriately and effectively by nonprofit organizations, can serve to improve organizational adaptability, leadership, and management, as well as the technical capacity to do the work.

What Is Evaluative Learning?

To make evaluation a cornerstone of organizational learning and capacity building may require a reexamination of the way one designs, conducts, and uses evaluation. This book describes an evaluation approach that is particularly useful for facilitating ongoing organizational learning. This approach may require a degree of compromise regarding the need for a completely objective evaluation and how the evaluation methodology is designed. Evaluations that maintain objectivity and only use outside evaluators are useful for accountability, but less so for organizational capacity building and learning. Additionally, these types of evaluations are often more expensive, thereby hindering an organization's or funder's ability to support evaluation. This is not to say that evaluations designed and implemented by an outside evaluator are not useful for organizational learning;

rather, these types of evaluations tend to have less buy-in from organizational leaders and stakeholders, and the findings focus on the client outcomes and the quality of the program—not the implications for the way the organization is functioning.

So what is evaluative learning?

Evaluative learning is an ongoing, collaboratively designed, and stakeholder-led evaluation process that has the primary purpose of serving organizational learning by evaluating the whole logic model.

Four principles illustrate the concept of evaluative learning:

1. Evaluate the whole logic model

2. Evaluation should be ongoing

3. Evaluations need to be collaboratively designed

4. Key stakeholders should lead the evaluation process

The definition also includes a fifth (and overarching) principle:

5. Organizational learning is the primary purpose of evaluative learning

1. Evaluate the whole logic model

The logic model is the best tool for evaluative learning. The W. K. Kellogg Foundation defines a *logic model* as "a systematic and visual way to present and share your understanding of the relationships among the resources you have to operate your program, the activities you plan to do, and the changes or results you hope to achieve."[vii] For the purposes of this book, the "resources you have to operate your program" are called *inputs,* the "activities you plan to do" are called *strategies,* and the "changes or results you hope to achieve" are called *outcomes* (if they refer directly to the recipients of services) and *impact* (if they refer to the change that occurs for the entire target population, of which the program recipients are a subset; impact is really community-level change). See the Sidebar, Evaluation Terms, page 10, for definitions.

Evaluation Terms

Here are some evaluation terms that you'll need to be familiar with as you read this book.

Evaluation: The systematic collection of information about the activities, characteristics, and outcomes of programs that specific people use to reduce uncertainties, improve effectiveness, and make decisions regarding what those programs are doing and affecting.[viii]

Formative evaluation: The process of integrating and using evaluation to develop and test programs and services with the goal of strengthening a program model on an ongoing basis. Ultimately, formative evaluation should lead to developing successful program models that could be replicated.

Summative evaluation: The use of evaluation to determine a program's success in achieving its intended outcomes. Ultimately, summative evaluation leads to the determination as to whether a program did what it was supposed to do. Summative evaluation is used primarily for accountability purposes.

Inputs: All the resources necessary for supporting a program; for example, money, time, expertise, experience, facilities, and technology.

Strategies: The specific activities, interventions, services, and programs that address specific needs or problems of a particular target audience; for example, case management services for homeless families, advocacy efforts for particular legislation, or policy changes that will improve the education system.

Outputs: A short-term measure of program strategy implementation; for example, number of clients served, number of services provided to clients, or actual dollar expenditures per client.

Outcomes: The short- and longer-term effects of program strategies on client behaviors, attitudes, knowledge, or perceptions; for example, whether students show improved performance in math coursework, or homeless clients obtain and maintain affordable housing.

Impact: The long-term and aggregate effect of a sustained program, service, or intervention on the overall target population.

Logic model: A conceptual depiction of the program inputs, strategies, outputs, outcomes, and impact, and the assumed causal relationship between them. The logic model serves as a planning, communication, and evaluation tool or framework.

So why is it important to use a logic model for the purposes of evaluative learning? When an organization develops a logic model, it is describing each of the logic model elements listed on page 9 (inputs, strategies, outcomes, and impact), as well as its assumptions about the causal relationship between each of these elements.[1] Arrows show the causal relationships in a logic model and indicate where evaluative learning is the greatest.

Figure 2, Example of a Logic Model, page 12, shows what the logic model would look like for the organization described earlier that is providing job opportunities for homeless individuals. This figure will help you see how concrete program activities can be described using a logic model. Figure 3, Evaluating the Whole Logic Model, page 13, shows the logic model in its abstract form, noting the types of evaluation questions that can be asked about each element of the model.

Overall, any evaluation will ask one or more of the following five questions:

1. Did our clients change, and if so, how much and in what ways?

2. How much service did we provide and what was the quality of that service?

3. What was the quantity and quality of the resources we used to implement our programs?

4. Which resources were most important for providing high-quality service?

5. Which strategies (program qualities) were most important for achieving the desired outcomes?

However, the highest level of evaluative learning occurs only when an organization closely examines the last two questions, which relate the organization's strategic choices to its outcomes and effectiveness. If one looks at any logic model, these last two questions relate to the arrows in the model. (See Figure 3, Evaluating the Whole Logic Model.)

---

[1] Many evaluators and organizations develop logic models without using arrows, instead presenting each of the logic model elements in table form. While it may be implicitly clear which inputs support which strategies, which strategies lead to which outcomes, and which outcomes lead to the impact, arrows help to make them explicit.

Figure 2. Example of a Logic Model

Below is a sample logic model, showing how one program modeled the way its inputs, strategies, and outputs resulted in outcomes and impact.

Inputs	Strategies	Outputs	Outcomes	Impact
All of the resources necessary for supporting a program	The specific activities, interventions, services, and/or programs that serve a particular target audience	A short-term measure of program strategy implementation	The short- and longer-term effects of program strategies on client behaviors, attitudes, knowledge, and/or perceptions	The long-term and ag-gregate effect of a sus-tained program, service, or intervention on the overall target population

- Funding
- Local transporta-tion authority bus ticket allocation
- Skills, knowledge, and experience of job trainers, job coaches, and support group facilitators
- Receptivity of employees
- Training materials
- Space
- Client motivation and willingness to support one another
- Client pre-exist-ing job skills and experience

Provide job training to homeless individuals → Fifty-five clients receive high-quality job training each year → Clients meet or exceed the skill requirements of the job for which they were trained

Provide transporta-tion to and from places of employment → Ten bus tickets per individual are provided weekly

Provide job coach-ing for the first six months of employment → Each client receives four hours of coach-ing per month → At least 90 percent of all clients hold their job for at least six months

Offer peer vocation-al support groups once a week for the first six months of employment → Each client attends at least one support group meeting per month

Decreased homelessness in the community

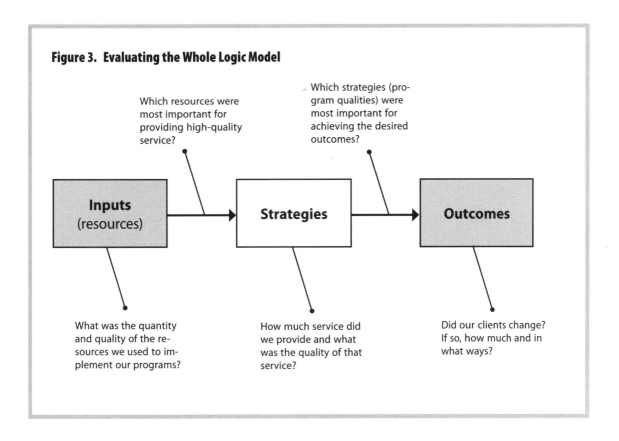

Figure 3. Evaluating the Whole Logic Model

Which resources were most important for providing high-quality service?

Which strategies (program qualities) were most important for achieving the desired outcomes?

Inputs (resources)

Strategies

Outcomes

What was the quantity and quality of the resources we used to implement our programs?

How much service did we provide and what was the quality of that service?

Did our clients change? If so, how much and in what ways?

Too often, evaluations only look at one of the logic model elements. For example, many funders engage an external evaluator to assess the outcomes of a grantmaking program. These funders may believe the only decision to be made about the success of their programs is whether those programs achieved their outcomes. Some funders may feel it is too costly, difficult, or time-consuming to conduct evaluations that look at the whole logic model, or they use evaluation only to determine grantee accountability.

If an evaluation doesn't examine the relationship between inputs, strategies, and outcomes (that is, the arrows), then it is impossible to examine cost-effectiveness. For example, let's say a funder invests $200,000 in a leadership development program, hoping that nonprofit executive directors will not leave the nonprofit sector. The program includes a yearlong peer exchange process with a group of local nonprofit leaders, as well as executive coaching. Through an external evaluation, the funder learns that in fact the executive directors in this program stay in the nonprofit sector longer than executive directors who are not in this program. However, because the evaluation only focused on the outcomes, and didn't consider the quality of the intervention or the resources used, the funder does not know how the program achieved this result. Was it the peer exchange process, the coaching, or some combination of both (that is, program strategies)? Was it the length of the intervention (again, strategies)? Was it the quality of peer exchange facilitators (a program input)?

Neither the funder nor the program provider can answer these critical questions, even though the outcome has been successful. Nor do they have the data to assess whether they could achieve the same success again, and perhaps for less cost. Had they examined the whole model, including the arrows, they might have learned how to save money from the effort, get the same result, and use the savings for other grantmaking efforts—perhaps to expand the program to serve more people.

Beginning the evaluative learning process by developing and agreeing to evaluate the whole logic model sets the stage for using evaluation as a capacity-building tool. This is the case for both nonprofit organizations and funders.

2. Evaluation should be ongoing

To best serve organizational learning, evaluation must be ongoing. Whether initiated by funders or nonprofit organizations, evaluations tend to occur periodically, if at all. When evaluation does occur, it is usually at a time when funders need to make critical grantmaking decisions or nonprofit organizations want to prove that their programs are worth new or continued support. The evaluation process needs to occur frequently, repeatedly, and in alignment with decisions on key organizational and programmatic concerns.

Let's take a closer look at what this means.

Nonprofits will need to determine when in the service delivery process they can best gather data on client outcomes, the quality of the program, and the quality of the resources used to run the programs. For many programs, nonprofits will not be able to gather resource, strategy, and outcome data all at the same time. In fact, nonprofits will typically need to gather data on the quality of programs and resources one or more times during the service delivery process, and perhaps at each point of direct intervention with the client. Nonprofits may need to collect outcome data prior to a client receiving services (baseline data), immediately following service delivery, and, in an ideal world, sometime after the client receives services (six months or one year, for example).

Many nonprofit organizations already collect some type of evaluation data, such as program outputs (measures of how much service was delivered, to whom, for how long, and with what frequency) and customer satisfaction data. However, even these types of data are often not analyzed frequently enough to provide maximum benefit to the organization. For example, an arts organization that provides art education classes to the community conducts a satisfaction survey following each class. Staff analyze the data at the end of each year to provide information to their funders. However, prior to the end of the year, the education staff met quarterly to plan classes for the subsequent quarter. Because they hadn't analyzed the current customer satisfaction data, they used the prior year's evaluation report, pulled and discussed examples from the current satisfaction surveys, and relied on the educators' anecdotal observations to make decisions during these meetings. If they had analyzed the data more frequently, their decisions could reflect more current trends.

Data must be collected and analyzed repeatedly if organizations are to benefit from it in the long run. Many nonprofits are able to acquire funding to support program evaluation. However, funders usually don't provide ongoing funding of evaluation. Thus, nonprofits may use the one-time evaluation findings for an extended period of time to make organizational and programmatic decisions even though the findings may no longer be relevant due to changes in programs, program staff, the problem being addressed, client characteristics, and other factors. Continuing to use the same tools, analysis processes, and reporting mechanisms will help an organization develop benchmarks for success, and thereby institutionalize the learning needed to monitor progress. One-time evaluations are like milk and bread—they have an expiration date, and it's always sooner than you hoped!

Funders usually don't provide ongoing funding of evaluation. One-time evaluations are like milk and bread—they have an expiration date, and it's always sooner than you hoped!

Finally, evaluative learning needs to be aligned with key programmatic and organizational decision making. Ongoing evaluative learning will be most useful when program changes are being decided. Evaluative learning answers the questions of whether, which, and how programs achieve success so an organization can learn what works, what doesn't, and why.

Evaluative learning can and should serve all organizational decision-making processes. When an organization's program evaluation assesses which resources are most important to ensuring achievement of desired outcomes, it will glean better insights for making organizational decisions, especially if the information is available at the time when decisions get made.

Let's say that an organization begins an evaluative learning process. This organization provides mentoring to teenage mothers by pairing former teenage mothers with new teenage mothers to provide information, knowledge, and emotional support. Through these evaluation efforts, the organization learns two key findings: (1) when the mentor takes the new mother and her baby on outings where the mentor, new mom, and baby participate in baby enrichment activities together (such as a play group), the new mother is more likely to pursue additional baby enrichment opportunities without the mentor; and (2) the mentors can only provide these opportunities once in a while because the organization doesn't have the money to pay for them nor access to free or subsidized enrichment programs.

This finding should prompt organizational leaders to decide on a strategy for obtaining the resources to support baby enrichment outings, either by seeking additional funds or by identifying other free or low-cost programs in the community that their clients could easily use. Organizational leaders could also use this information to shift resources to similar opportunities, as well as inspire staff and mentors to use more baby enrichment programs. It may even inspire leaders to create a new program. With respect to adaptive capacity, these findings should encourage organizational staff members to collaborate and network with other service providers who have these programs or could become partners in developing a new program. From a management perspective, program managers need to ensure that mentors get the resources (adequate notice, money, transportation) they need to sign up for baby enrichment opportunities, as well as the training that mentors need to make best use of the baby enrichment activities. The mentor training will in turn improve the mentors' skills, knowledge, and experience (a technical capacity) to make sure that the mother and child benefit from the enrichment.

Without timely evaluation findings, these decisions might never get made, the organization likely wouldn't create the kind of change it needed, managers might not make best use of the mentors, and mentors wouldn't provide the kinds of enrichment that could make a difference in these teenage mothers' lives.

3. Evaluations need to be collaboratively designed

Successful evaluative learning requires broad buy-in. When organizational leaders, staff, partners, funders, and constituents all engage in designing the evaluation, they become active participants in shaping what and how they want to learn, and as a result are much more likely to use what they learn.

Any evaluation process includes the following steps. To maximize evaluative learning, it is critically important to collaboratively involve key stakeholders during each of these evaluation steps.

1. Develop the logic model

2. Identify the key evaluation questions using the logic model

3. Determine the evidence stakeholders would say represents adequate answers to the evaluation questions (the "indicators")

4. Develop data collection methods

5. Develop an evaluative learning plan that identifies the evaluation question, indicators, method, tasks, and individuals responsible for each task

During step one, the development of the logic model, many typical evaluation efforts engage an external evaluator or one or two organizational or programmatic leaders. Since the logic model makes explicit all of the assumptions about the program, it is critically important to get input, feedback, and validation for the logic model from all those individuals inside and outside of the organization who have a stake in the program (such as community leaders, funders, and clients). A collaborative logic model development process that engages all key stakeholders grounds the evaluation design in everyone's assumptions about the program's goals and methods. In addition, the collaborative process itself serves as the beginning of the evaluative learning process. As stakeholders reconcile their differences of opinion about what the program should be doing, how it should be doing it, and the changes it should be affecting, individuals learn how other key stakeholders view the program. Additionally, the collaborative logic model development process brings people together around a common set of assumptions, which not only improves the evaluation design, but also how those individuals understand and do their work.

In step two, stakeholders identify the key evaluation questions. Because of their high engagement in the logic model development process, stakeholders may have already begun identifying evaluation questions. It is therefore important to continue the evaluative learning process by formally and collaboratively eliciting these priority questions. This ensures that the evaluative learning process addresses these questions, thereby maximizing stakeholder buy-in to and commitment for implementing and using the evaluation. If stakeholders don't have the opportunity to put forth their own priority evaluation questions, many will find the evaluation findings irrelevant to their roles and responsibilities to the organization—especially those to whom the evaluation findings seem "critical "or negative.

Steps three and four identify the types of evidence (or indicators) that one would expect to see if programs are high quality and the outcomes are achieved, as well as the methods that will best serve to collect this evidence. Typically, this is where organizations rely heavily on an external evaluator, with minimal input from organizational leaders. However, it is critically important to collaboratively engage representatives of key stakeholders. Without such stakeholder involvement, an external evaluator may develop a set of measures or indicators and methodologies that are strong from a research design standpoint, but that key stakeholders believe are inappropriate given the context of their programs and organization. The result: stakeholders may view the findings as irrelevant and dismiss evaluation as not helpful. It is fine and appropriate to engage an external evaluator to provide technical assistance and advice about measures or indicators and data collection methods. However, stakeholders need to collaboratively make final decisions about the appropriate measures or indicators and data collection methods.

Step five, developing and implementing an evaluation work plan, is typically delegated to an external evaluator. However, in an evaluative learning process, it is important for stakeholders to collaboratively develop and implement the evaluation work plan. Collaborative development ensures that stakeholders self-identify tasks they will implement for the evaluation—which improves accountability for completing the plan. Additionally, it gives stakeholders a say as to the feasibility and validity of data collection methods—which increases the likelihood that they will execute the work plan. Of course, even with collaborative development, stakeholders may need an external evaluator's technical assistance in the evaluation planning and implementation process, for such tasks as collecting and analyzing data, and writing or cowriting the evaluation findings.

An example of a collaborative process follows.

The Massachusetts Cultural Council (MCC) sought to develop an evaluation plan for its START Initiative, a program to provide organizational capacity-building assistance to local cultural councils and arts and cultural organizations throughout the state. This client engaged an outside evaluator to serve as a facilitator and provide evaluation technical assistance, but not to serve as the evaluator. MCC wanted expert help with specific methodological issues, but also wanted to ensure that the evaluation addressed its ongoing learning needs. MCC asked *all program staff* to participate in a number of meetings that the outside evaluator facilitated and that laid out the logic model, questions, methods, and indicators. Organizational leaders and staff proposed the evaluation questions, methods, and indicators, while the evaluation consultant provided feedback regarding feasibility and helped ensure that the research design addressed its long-term learning goals.

As a direct result of this client-led approach, each of the program staff members came away from the process with a clear sense of how the evaluation would meet their specific learning needs and with ideas about how they would use the findings to improve their work. Once the system is in place, every participant will have a stake in making sure the evaluation occurs in a high-quality fashion.

4. Key stakeholders should lead the evaluation process

By definition, key stakeholders are those individuals who have a stake in an organization or its programs and services. Not everyone has an equal stake, therefore each person's role in the evaluative learning process is different. The critical point is that when stakeholders *lead* an evaluation process (make informed final decisions about what to do to implement the plan, when to implement action steps, and whether to conduct certain evaluation processes) they are much more likely to use the findings to make plans and decisions.

The evaluation consultant provides expertise and advice on *how* to conduct the evaluation; *options* for data collection, analysis, and report writing; and direct data collection and analysis *support*. For example, if an organization decides to conduct focus groups with program participants, it will get more candid information by having an outside consultant conduct the focus groups. Additionally, regarding data analysis, an evaluator has likely had more training and experience with both qualitative and quantitative data analysis. Therefore, an evaluation consultant would likely save time, provide more accurate findings, and conduct more detailed analyses than the organization could.

The organization, once provided the consultant's advice, options, and support, should decide which steps will best serve the learning goals of the process. The nonprofit should *lead* the process. In many nonprofit organizations, executive directors may not have the expertise to conduct the day-to-day financial management of their organization, yet they still make the financial decisions. If internal evaluation capacity is lacking, an outside consultant should *manage* the process.[2]

For example, the Strategic Solutions Initiative, a jointly funded five-year initiative with the goal of improving the understanding and use of strategic restructuring among funders, consultants, and nonprofit leaders, conducted an evaluation of its efforts. Its core strategies included conducting research and sharing what was learned, training consultants on how to facilitate strategic restructuring processes, and disseminating knowledge locally and nationally through workshops and presentations. Evaluation was a part of this initiative from the beginning. The funders—the James Irvine Foundation, the David and Lucile Packard Foundation, and the William and Flora Hewlett Foundation—and the grantee, La Piana Associates, jointly designed the evaluation plan with the assistance of an outside evaluator. While implementing the plan, key stakeholders from these organizations also made all final decisions as to which of the consultant's

[2] For a helpful discussion of the role of a consultant in evaluation, see *The Manager's Guide to Program Evaluation: Planning, Contracting, and Managing for Useful Results* by Paul Mattessich, available from Fieldstone Alliance.

data collection and analysis options would be implemented. Additionally, these stakeholders all provided leadership regarding how the data could and should be interpreted.

As a result of their involvement, the stakeholders "owned" the findings. For example, when the data showed that not enough was known about the role leadership played in a nonprofit's decision to consider strategic restructuring, the stakeholders revised the initiative's strategies to address this gap in knowledge. These changes in strategy would have been less likely if all stakeholders were not leading the evaluation process. Having stakeholders play a leading role in interpreting the findings ensures that learning opportunities aren't overlooked.

5. Organizational learning is the primary purpose of evaluative learning

Evaluative learning serves ongoing internal program and organizational planning and development *before* it serves accountability to others. As a result, the evaluative learning process requires a shift away from focusing on understanding what went wrong and toward an understanding of what works and how to strengthen it further. In short, the shift from accountability to learning requires a shift away from looking for problems and toward looking for solutions.

> The evaluative learning process requires a shift away from focusing on understanding what went wrong and toward an understanding of what works and how to strengthen it further.

Too many times outcome-based evaluations only tell a small part of the story: whether participants changed the way we wanted them to. When evaluation efforts include assessing the relationships between inputs, strategies, and outcomes, we learn that some things worked and some things did not, and we get some good ideas about *why*. Evaluative learning, because of its focus on telling the whole story (using all of the logic model elements, including the arrows), often forces nonprofit organizations *and* their funders to come face-to-face with the fact that no program is completely working or completely not working. It then becomes tougher to decide whether to "pull the plug" on a program and, instead, forces everyone to invest more energy and resources toward strengthening the things that work. In the end evaluative learning may help funders and nonprofits create programs that work, share "best practices," and ultimately develop strategies for replicating successful programs. In fact, evaluative learning may prove that some things work, some things don't, and most things could be improved with more time and a better use of resources.

Summary

Key points in this chapter:

- Evaluation is a critical capacity for becoming a true learning organization. An ongoing and thoughtful evaluation process or system is the key to making effective and mission-based organizational decisions.

- A nonprofit needs four core capacities—leadership, management, adaptive capacity, and technical capacity—and ongoing evaluation should serve each of these four capacities.

- Evaluative learning is an ongoing, collaboratively designed, and stakeholder-led evaluation process having the primary purpose of serving organizational learning. Learning is maximized when an organization evaluates the entire logic model.

Chapter Two

How Evaluative Learning
Builds Capacity

T O IMPLEMENT AN EVALUATIVE LEARNING PROCESS, funders and nonprofit organizations will need to partner together so the learning can serve everyone. This will require each funder to take a close and hard look at their beliefs, values, and assumptions as to *why* and *how* they evaluate their grantmaking. To further explore these issues, this chapter will present the following:

- Why and how funders typically evaluate their grantees' programs

- How funders' reasons and methods differ from the reasons and methods that nonprofits (the grantees) use to evaluate their programs

- How evaluative learning can serve as a bridge to improve the capacity and effectiveness of *both* grantmakers and nonprofits

As this section explores why and how funders typically evaluate their grantmaking, it is *not* referring to why and how funders evaluate their own grantmaking process (the development of grantmaking programs, the funder's stewardship of resources, and the relationship between potential or actual grantees and the funder), but rather the quality and outcomes of the grantee-implemented programs that their dollars fund. Also, this section will refer to "grantmaking programs" and "initiatives"; for the purposes of this book these terms are synonymous, and refer to program grants made to multiple nonprofits that in turn use the funds to implement programs that address a particular personal, social, or community challenge.

How Funders Typically Use Evaluation

Funders most often use evaluation for purposes of accountability. However, if evaluation were conducted in a way that benefited both funders' and non-profits' ongoing learning needs, it could demonstrate accountability *and* build capacity. The end result would be an overall improvement in grantmaking, as well as the ability of the nonprofit sector to better achieve success.

Evaluation often comes in the form of an unfunded demand that grantees measure success. As a result, grantees really aren't learning from their evaluation efforts; rather, they are grudgingly doing what they are told.

It seems that most funders throughout the country do not *formally* evaluate the effectiveness of their grants. However, this is not to say that funders are not asking evaluative questions of their grantmaking and their grantees. In fact, many funders informally evaluate their grantmaking daily: they request progress reports from their grantees at the end of the grant, they make site visits to grantee organizations to assess the effectiveness of their programs, and otherwise try to find out if their grantmaking goals were met.

In the past, the anecdotal evidence gained from these methods satisfied many funders. In evaluation terms, this evidence was proof of the "outputs." However, due to increasing government and public pressure on the nonprofit sector to prove impact and the legitimacy of its claim to a tax-exempt status,[ix] more and more funders are now focusing on and, in many cases, are only interested in, the "outcomes." As a result, the once-satisfactory informal evaluation of the outputs is no longer enough. The funders' typical response is to instruct their grantees to provide proof of outcomes at the close of the grant. The implication for grantees is that they have to somehow—often without the technical skills, knowledge, or resources—evaluate their program outcomes. So evaluation often comes in the form of an unfunded demand that grantees measure success. As a result, grantees really aren't learning from their evaluation efforts; rather, they are grudgingly doing what they are told.

Does the drive for accountability interfere with learning?

Many large foundations often use more formal evaluation approaches, and most do so for purposes of accountability. In a 1998 study of fourteen national foundations and seven regional foundations, researchers Patricia Patrizi and Bernard McMullan asked funders about the purpose of their evaluation efforts.[x] The study found that "high priority is given to using evaluation to strengthen grantee, foundation, and field practice." This finding seems to contradict the statement that most large foundations evaluate for the purpose of accountability. However, when foundations in this study were asked who the key constituencies were for their evaluations, they named the top three priority constituencies as foundation board, foundation staff, and foundation management. Grantees were the fourth highest priority constituency, but foundations in this study were split as to whether grantees were a top or secondary priority.

Perhaps larger foundations want to place a high value on using evaluation as a tool to support the improvement of their grantees' work, but have not actualized this value. And one of the main reasons the study cites is that foundation boards increasingly put a higher premium on both achieving the desired outcomes for their foundation's grantmaking and on being able to attribute these outcomes directly to their grantmaking.

It is safe to say that if funders were asked, How would you evaluate your grantmaking if money were no object? many would respond that a control group study with random assignment is the best approach, and that an outside evaluator should conduct a rigorous evaluation. However, the reality is that cost does matter, and such rigor is expensive. The key point here is not an argument against using rigorous evaluation designs, but rather a reassessment of the purpose that the evaluation design serves. In the academic world, social researchers apply rigorous scientific methods to study social problems for the purpose of furthering knowledge—in other words, the purpose of research is learning. However, in the funder and evaluation communities,

> In the funder and evaluation communities, the purpose of evaluation is primarily about accountability, because critical decisions have to be made about how to spend a limited amount of money—about *which* grantees should get funded.

the purpose of evaluation is primarily about accountability because critical decisions have to be made about how to spend a limited amount of money—about *which* grantees should get funded.

Funders can change this purpose. They can shift the focus of evaluation away from accountability *only* and toward using evaluation as a learning and capacity-building tool that serves both funders and grantees. As such, there will necessarily be a level of compromise on the evaluation design. That's nothing new—scientific rigor often is compromised due to financial constraints, ethical issues related to the use of human subjects, and a lack of research expertise.

Funders should consider three questions with respect to this compromise:

1. How much of your grant portfolio are you currently evaluating using a rigorous design and an outside evaluator?

2. If you are evaluating some of your grants using this approach, have the findings met your foundation's accountability needs?

3. If you are not evaluating your grants using an outside evaluator and rigorous methods, are you receiving reports and data from your grantees that meet your accountability needs?

Most funders find that they are not evaluating their grants using an outside evaluator who applies scientific methodologies, nor do they have the money to do so. Additionally, regarding the quality of reports from grantees, most funders would likely say that all they hear about are what the grantees did, and not about the impact their grantees' efforts had on the problem being addressed.

The important question here is, How much learning is *really* happening from evaluation efforts for the funders, the grantees, and the field? What can you change to be sure that evaluation dollars result in better practices?

How Nonprofits Typically Use Evaluation

There still is a dearth of research in the field regarding how nonprofits conduct and use evaluation. One thing is clear—a large majority of nonprofit organizations do not conduct rigorous evaluations using scientific methods for one of three main reasons:

1. Nonprofits do not have the funds to develop and implement these methodologies, either by themselves or using an outside evaluator.

2. Nonprofits do not have staff with the research skills to conduct these types of evaluations.

3. Nonprofit leaders and their staff don't see this type of design as of high value to themselves or their stakeholders.

In 1991, researchers conducted an exploratory study of how nonprofits apply evaluation and found that rigorously designed evaluations have not been successful in evaluating human service programs because these formal approaches were not responsive to the interests and concerns of stakeholders.[xi]

Like funders, nonprofit organizations use evaluation for the purposes of accountability.

So why and how do nonprofits conduct evaluation? In 1998, the Innovation Network studied program evaluation practices in the nonprofit sector.[xii] This study found that evaluations are primarily conducted for current funders, and that these evaluations are focused on outcome measurement, which the authors of the study point out "is a fairly recent practice that is continuing to grow." This is a clear indication that like funders, nonprofit organizations use evaluation for the purposes of accountability. Additionally, this study pointed out that nearly half of all the nonprofits conducting evaluations stated that they are evaluating outcomes as a requirement of their funding—again, indicating that evaluations are being conducted for external reasons.

The Role Evaluation *Should* Play in Organizational Capacity Building

Using evaluation for accountability purposes is fine. But for little extra effort, evaluation can be part of a step-by-step organizational learning process. The phases in the learning process are

Phase 1: Knowledge gathering

Phase 2: Organizational planning

Phase 3: Program planning

Phase 4: Program implementation

Phase 5: Repeat

Figure 4, A Model of Organizational Learning, provides a picture of this model.

Phase 1: Knowledge gathering

All organizational learning begins with gathering the knowledge needed to make planning decisions. To be effective, all nonprofit organizations need to be what many in the field call "learning organizations." A *learning organization* is a nonprofit that consistently and regularly gathers, analyzes, and uses information to serve *all* organizational and program planning. Using the model of organizational effectiveness described in Chapter 1, a true learning organization has a high degree of adaptive capacity—the ability to monitor, assess, respond to, and create internal and external changes.

Organizational learning occurs through many means:

- *Networking and partnering with others in the community.* Nonprofits gather a significant amount of information about the policies, programs, and other environmental factors affecting their work through meeting with community leaders, including nonprofit, government, and for-profit business leaders. This information is invaluable to organizational and program planning and decision making.

Figure 4. A Model of Organizational Learning

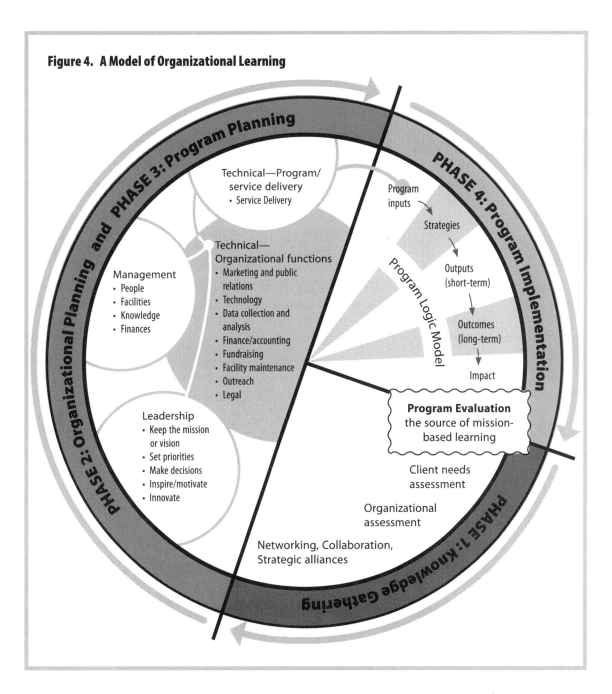

- *Organizational assessment.* Nonprofit organizations gather information formally through conducting organizational assessments of their effectiveness (for example, through the strategic planning process of identifying the organization's strengths, weaknesses, opportunities, and threats; by conducting a formal organizational assessment using tools designed by the research or consulting community; and by other means). They also assess their organizations informally through meetings and communication with managers and staff members. Formal or informal, these assessments provide valuable information for the organization's plans and decisions.

- *Client needs assessment.* Nonprofit organizations often conduct needs assessments of their target population to inform programs and plans. Some nonprofits do this informally or anecdotally by talking with current clients and documenting their needs. Other organizations conduct formal needs assessments using research methods like focus groups, interviews, and surveys.

- *Program evaluation.* Nonprofit organizations often informally and formally (or more rigorously) evaluate their programs by monitoring how much service is delivered (the "outputs"), assessing client satisfaction or program quality, or client short- and long-term outcomes. Program evaluation findings ideally provide critical mission-based information and knowledge that guide both programmatic and organizational decisions.

A nonprofit achieves its mission through its programs and services. Program evaluation is therefore one of the best tools an organization can use to better understand its success at achieving its mission.

Phase 2: Organizational planning

Once an organization has synthesized all the information gathered through all learning processes, it needs to use the information for organizational planning. *Organizational planning* is a process that organizational leaders facilitate, and that serves to make strategic decisions about how to acquire, allocate, efficiently use, and be accountable for effectively spending all organizational resources. Organizations need to make specific decisions that provide clear direction to managers on how to make efficient and effective use of the organization's human, facilities, knowledge, and financial resources. Managers then need to direct and oversee staff who in turn will carry out the organization's technical functions (marketing, public relations, technology, data collection and analysis, finance and accounting, fundraising, facility maintenance, outreach, legal, and so forth).

The organization's technical functions all serve to support (or, in evaluation terminology, serve as resources or inputs for) program delivery. For example:

- The *marketing* function will lead to new human or financial resources that will, at least in part, be put toward program implementation.

- The *technology* function will give direct service providers the knowledge or efficient process for working most effectively with their clients.

- *Facility maintenance* will ensure that clients receive services in a space that is usable and set up to maximize the benefits of the services.

While providing necessary resources for program delivery, the organization's technical functions also provide resources for sustaining the organization. For example, the technical function of fundraising can provide dollars both for programs (resources for carrying out the mission) and for general operating support (resources for sustaining the organizational process).

Effective organizational planning and decision making requires solid information to fully answer the question, How can we strengthen our organization to achieve our mission? Program evaluation is the best learning tool for providing this information. To get this information, the organization needs to conduct ongoing program evaluation of all programs—especially evaluation that closely examines how the quantity and quality of all program resources affect the quality of program strategies. If one thinks of the organization's mission as a big-picture snapshot of the desired client outcomes and impact on the community, the best way to "measure mission" is to routinely evaluate program outcomes. So, program evaluation is one of the best learning tools for organizational planning because it both measures mission (client outcomes) and provides information to organizational leaders about resources that support the most effective program strategies.

Phase 3: Program planning

Program planning entails making decisions about how to best use organizational resources to maximize the quantity and quality of program delivery. It specifically entails allocating resources based on a clear understanding of what specific program elements achieve the greatest amount of benefit for the largest number of clients. To make these decisions, program evaluation needs to focus on answering the question, Which particular program components, processes, or delivery mechanisms are most highly associated with or definitively result in clients achieving the desired outcomes? As discussed earlier, this is a logic model "arrow" question—a question derived from the arrows depicted in the logic model that connect specific strategies with specific outcomes. (See Figure 3. Evaluating the Whole Logic Model on page 13) Adequately addressing this program planning question requires a program evaluation that measures both the quantity and quality of strategy implementation and client outcomes.

Let's take an example of a drug and alcohol counseling center that works with court-referred clients. This center is conducting a program evaluation of its one-to-one counseling services. As part of this evaluation, the center asks all clients to anonymously complete a survey of questions about the quality of the counseling sessions, including the quality of their relationship with their counselor. Court mandates also require random testing of these clients for alcohol and drug use. So, this evaluation is gathering both strategy (service delivery) data and outcome data. When the data are analyzed, the center finds that the perceived quality of the communication and interpersonal skills of the counselors and the counselors' ability to connect clients with outside resources for additional support (like support groups or recovering individuals to provide one-to-one support) are more highly correlated with clean alcohol and drug tests. However, no correlation exists between amount of time that the counselor spends providing alcohol and drug education and alcohol and drug test results.

Armed with these findings, the center decides during program planning to encourage counselors to spend less time on education and more time directly communicating with clients, as well as more time providing information about external support resources. This is a reallocation of a program input—staff time. The center also decides to recruit a volunteer to develop and maintain a database of all external support resources available in the community. This is a resource decision, since it results in recruiting new human resources (the volunteer), and shifting (or acquiring) financial resources to develop the technology needed to build the database. Without conducting a program evaluation that explicitly examines the relationship between the quantity and quality of services (the counseling intervention) and the client outcomes (negative alcohol and drug tests), resource decisions would have been difficult and likely based on anecdote and gut experience.

Phase 4: Program implementation

Once the learning and planning are completed, the programs need to be implemented. By evaluating the programs and using the findings for organizational and program planning, one should expect the programs to be more successful because more resources are allocated for critical program components—the best practices that will make a real difference.

Phase 5: Repeat

Evaluative learning is ongoing. Evaluations should be conducted in a cycle, with information gleaned from one evaluation used to improve processes that will be evaluated in the next. Real learning will take place when the organization gets accustomed to continuous evaluation, and to applying the knowledge it gains from each evaluation cycle.

The most important point to take away from the evaluative learning process is that if an organization isn't conducting logic model-focused program evaluations (that is, evaluating the inputs, strategies, and outcomes, and the arrows in between) on an ongoing basis, organizational and programmatic planning will lack the necessary information to answer the key leadership and decision-making question, Are we closer to achieving our mission?

Table 1, Use of Evaluation to Improve Organizational Capacity, presents some strategies nonprofits can employ to use evaluation findings to improve key organizational functions and capacities.

Table 1. Use of Evaluation to Improve Organizational Capacity

How nonprofits can use evaluation to improve organizational capacity	Organizational capacity improvement
Incorporate evaluation findings into *all* planning activities	Strategic planning and leadership development and all other organizational capacities
Share evaluation findings with staff	Human resource and program development
Use evaluation findings to affirm the work of staff	Human resource development
Share evaluation findings with volunteers	Human resource development
Train board members to integrate evaluation into decision making	Board development
Incorporate evaluation findings in board meeting	Governance and leadership development
Share evaluation findings with clients	Program development
Share evaluation findings with funders	Fundraising
Use evaluation findings to strengthen grant proposals	Fundraising
Share evaluation findings with the community	Marketing and communication
Incorporate evaluation findings into financial decision making	Financial management

Summary

Key points in this chapter:

- When funders support evaluation, it most often serves accountability needs. Over the past few years, the trend has shifted away from accountability for what a nonprofit has implemented and toward evaluating client outcomes. Yet, nonprofits typically lack the technical skills and resources to conduct these types of evaluations. Additionally, these types of evaluation efforts often don't respond to the types of questions that will most benefit organizational learning.

- When nonprofit organizations conduct evaluations, they also often do so for accountability purposes. When they evaluate their programs, more and more nonprofits focus their efforts on the outcomes, reinforcing the use of evaluation for accountability. However, most nonprofits do not formally evaluate their programs because they lack the money, time, and skills to do so.

- Evaluation should play a critical role in organizational learning. In fact, evaluation is a critically important learning tool that allows an organization to gain a clearer understanding of its progress toward achieving its mission. Armed with evaluation findings, organizations can plan more effectively and deliver programs and services in a manner that maximizes impact.

In the next chapter, we'll look at how grantmakers can shift their strategies to meet their goals while furthering evaluative learning.

Chapter Three

Grantmaker and Grantee: Partners in Evaluative Learning

A CRITICAL STEP FOR FUNDERS THAT SUPPORT USING evaluation as a capacity-building tool is not a particular task, but rather a change in philosophy as to the reasons for conducting evaluation, how evaluation should be employed, and why. This chapter will describe this necessary shift.

As noted in Chapter 2, an accountability focus on outcomes evaluation is often at odds with the skill, experience, and capacity nonprofits have to conduct these types of evaluation, and a singular focus on outcomes doesn't maximize learning. But a philosophy of evaluative learning can set the stage for funders and nonprofits to partner for learning. However, this win-win approach to evaluation is not without its compromises. In the end, both funders and nonprofits will not only learn a lot from the process, but will also walk away with more effective programs. To meet in the middle, both funders and nonprofits will need to make some concessions.

Perceptions of evaluation among nonprofits and funders are often dissimilar. Many funders and nonprofit leaders differ on the purpose of evaluation, what to evaluate, how to evaluate, who should evaluate, when to evaluate, and how to use findings. Since these are all critical questions to any evaluation process, exploring how funders and nonprofits differ in their answers can help provide a model for them to come together.

Any time evaluation is being considered the following questions need to be answered:

- Why should a program be evaluated?
- What should be evaluated?
- How should evaluation be conducted?
- Who should conduct the evaluation?
- When should an evaluation be conducted?
- How should the evaluation findings be used?

The next section of this book will examine how funders and nonprofit organizations typically respond to each of these questions, as well as how both can "partner" better for learning.

Why Should a Program Be Evaluated?

Funder response: Typically funders will state that they want to know if grantees have done what they said they would. Nonprofit organizations usually meet this purpose through monitoring and reporting on program outputs like the number of people served, the number of services or programs delivered, the frequency of service delivery, or descriptions of who was served. However, more and more funders, and especially their boards of trustees, are no longer satisfied with just the outputs. Additionally, nonprofits learn little about their programs and even less about their organizations because output data cannot provide details on what works and what doesn't. By focusing primarily on outcomes data, funders put themselves in a position to learn less about "best practices." It is difficult to know for sure what works without an understanding of how much and what quality of strategies achieved the outcomes.

Nonprofit response: Typically nonprofits state that they have to evaluate their programs as a condition of their funding. More recently, nonprofits also state that they want to know if their programs are making a difference (achieving the desired outcomes). In this way, nonprofits are beginning to view the evaluation of outcomes in a similar light as funders—outcomes will help them know if they are succeeding. Although evaluating outcomes is critical for evaluative learning to occur, conducting "outcomes-only" evaluations may do a poor job of looking at the quantity and quality of programs and services in relation to those outcomes. As a result, evaluative learning, or learning what works and why, is minimal.

Partnering for learning: The ideal answer from both funders and nonprofits would be that evaluation should serve program planning and improvement for funders and nonprofits, as well as organizational planning and effectiveness for nonprofit organizations.

What Should Be Evaluated?

Funder response: As already noted, funders typically answer that they desire to evaluate the outcomes of the programs they have funded. It is important to further examine what funders often mean when they talk about outcomes. With any grantmaking program or initiative, there will be a set of short- and long-term outcomes that are expected to be accomplished. For example, a funder has developed a grantmaking initiative focused on math-teacher professional development that seeks the following short-term outcomes: improved knowledge and understanding of the best pedagogical approaches to teaching math, improved substantive knowledge of math, and an increase in the number of professional colleagues to turn to for professional support. The program seeks the following long-term outcomes: application of best math-teaching practices in the classroom and improved student academic performance in math. Evaluating the short-term outcomes is likely easier than the long-term outcomes, because the long-term outcomes require tracking teachers postintervention. However, the funder wants to evaluate the long-term outcomes because telling a story about improved teaching behavior and student performance is more powerful than telling a story that only shares how teachers improved their knowledge, awareness, and understanding of pedagogical approaches. This funder's desire to measure the long-term outcomes is not uncommon, and in fact would be great. Unfortunately, long-term outcomes require long-term evaluation, the ability to track clients, and rigorous evaluation design and methodologies. Nonprofit organizations usually lack the capacity to provide long-term outcome data without a considerable investment of resources and some outside help.

> Long-term outcomes require long-term evaluation, the ability to track clients, and rigorous evaluation design and methodologies. Nonprofit organizations usually lack the capacity to provide long-term outcome data without a considerable investment of resources and some outside help.

Nonprofit response: While nonprofits definitely care about client outcomes, they view measuring client outcomes as more important to their funders and other external constituents. Almost all nonprofit leaders believe in their programs' ability to affect the desired outcomes and therefore don't feel a strong need to prove anything to themselves. After all, most nonprofit leaders have spent a considerable amount of time understanding client needs and designing services with client outcomes in the forefront of their minds. Therefore, outcomes measurement may seem unnecessary except to respond to external accountability. When nonprofits are deciding what to evaluate, they are primarily interested in ensuring that their programs are being fully implemented. The focus on evaluating the program outputs results from the need to make critical organizational decisions about resource use—if programs aren't being implemented at the appropriate level, organizational leaders and managers want to know why and how to shift resources to ensure that programs are efficiently and effectively implemented.

Partnering for learning: The ideal answer to the question of what to evaluate would be the entire program logic model. However, where funders would focus on the long-term outcomes, it would be more appropriate, feasible, and practical to focus on the short-term outcomes. Since short-term outcomes are the prerequisites for long-term behavior changes, they best serve to easily and quickly measure what about the services is working—the arrow between strategies and outcomes. To provide the greatest learning, nonprofits should measure the program quantity (outputs) and qualities, as well as the short-term outcomes. And they should measure the resources—time, money, expertise, experience, facilities, and knowledge—needed to implement the program strategies most critical to achieving short-term outcomes. Though perhaps not as directly beneficial to funders, this is critically important to nonprofits if they are to make the most effective resource decisions. By evaluating the relationship between resources and high-quality strategy implementation, funders too will be able to better answer the question as to how much it really costs to achieve the desired outcomes. In turn, funders and nonprofits will obtain the information they need to make the case for funding all program and overhead expenses.

How Should Evaluation Be Conducted?

Funder response: If possible, funders want to conduct evaluations that are designed using social science research methodologies, including the use of control or comparison groups. This design is the ideal choice because it can most accurately determine if a program or service caused an outcome. Additionally, if a control or comparison group study determines there is a cause-and-effect relationship, then the program can likely be replicated. This design answers two questions: Did the program work? Can the program work with other organizations or other communities?

However, funders often realize that a rigorous evaluation design requires more money, time, expertise, and research skills than either they or their grantees have. Also, denying services to members of a target population of clients (that is, establishing a control group) presents many ethical challenges—even if those services will eventually be delivered to all clients. At the same time, self-reports and grantee anecdotes of client outcomes are not highly valued because, understandably, they present a biased picture of a program's benefits. Additionally, these types of evaluations do not definitively establish some level of cause and effect, or at least a correlation between programs and client outcomes. Funders also prefer a mixed method design where both quantitative and qualitative data are collected, analyzed, and presented.

Nonprofit response: Nonprofits, understandably, want to conduct evaluations that are sensitive to their organizational and community context, as well as the realities of their clients' lives. As such, they show a strong preference for evaluation designs that include methods to collect subjective data, or individual "stories," from their clients. Nonprofit organizations often resist control or comparison group studies, fearing that the level of outcome won't be realized and that the evaluation will not take into account the environmental or other uncontrollable factors that might have led to a lesser result than envisioned. Unless the evaluation design is true random assignment of clients into two groups (one receiving the programs, one not), nonprofits are justified in their fears. Nonprofits also resist collecting only quantitative data, believing that the changes they are trying to affect are too difficult to measure only with numbers, and that numbers won't be able to tell the whole story. Funders' increased use of mixed-method designs indicates some agreement on this point. To gather more "context-specific" data, nonprofits are taking to mixed methodologies, using both quantitative and qualitative data collection methods.

Partnering for learning: Funders need to let go of the expectation that they will be able to scientifically prove that a program made a difference and that they can, someday, replicate a program (unless this is their specific purpose for funding a program). Nonprofits need to let go of the belief that their organizational and programmatic context is so unique that some set of objective measures of program quality and outcomes can't be developed. Next, nonprofits and funders need to engage in more dialogue and interaction to develop a set of mutually agreed-upon evaluation questions that meet everyone's accountability, planning, and learning needs. Finally, they both need to agree on the types of evidence (measures) that would satisfactorily answer the evaluation questions for either group.

From these agreed-upon evaluation questions and measures, funders and nonprofits can usually reach some compromise on the evaluation design and methodologies. If this dialogue doesn't or can't happen, it is important that both funders and nonprofits at least agree on an evaluation design that strives to gather both objective and subjective data using a research design that will best serve the purpose of improving learning for everyone.

Who Should Conduct the Evaluation?

Funder response: While often asking their grantees to evaluate their programs, most funders would like an external evaluator to conduct the evaluation—believing in the need for the application of social science research design and that a trained and experienced evaluator can bring this type of design to the work. Note that it is mostly only the large foundations that have the resources to conduct an external evaluation of some of their grantmaking initiatives or grantees. As such, funders usually leave it to the nonprofit to either hire an external evaluator (which they often don't have the resources to do), or conduct the evaluation themselves (which, understandably, leaves the funder questioning the objectivity and validity of the findings). Also, when nonprofits conduct their own evaluation, they often don't go beyond tracking program outputs, for the reasons cited earlier.

Nonprofit response: Ideally, nonprofit organizations would like to design and conduct the evaluation with their own staff. The reality is that they don't have the time or staff to do this. However, most nonprofits recognize the need for engaging outside assistance for evaluation design and data collection and analysis because they understand that outside assistance brings credibility, objectivity, client confidentiality during data collection and research, and analysis skills that the nonprofit often lacks. If they had the resources and a belief in the learning benefits of evaluation—and if they had the money—many nonprofits would hire an in-house evaluator so that all evaluation efforts would consider organizational and environmental context issues.

Partnering for learning: To achieve evaluative learning, there will likely need to be a partnership between nonprofits and external evaluators, especially when an organization doesn't have the resources to hire a full-time evaluator or has a strong need for objectivity. External evaluators can provide technical assistance and advice on designing ongoing evaluation efforts, assist in data collection where confidentiality or the appearance of objectivity is important, assist in data analysis when organizations don't have the qualitative or quantitative analysis skills, and provide professional development to in-house evaluators. External evaluators should not be the evaluation's sole designer and implementer if it is to serve evaluative learning. Instead, evaluators should provide a range of options that best addresses program and organizational learning needs and allow nonprofits to make the final decision on what will get implemented. Finally, when interpreting the findings, evaluators need to facilitate dialogue among organizational stakeholders (community, clients, staff, board, and funders) that helps these stakeholders understand what the evaluation information means for them and how they can act on it.

When Should an Evaluation Be Conducted?

Funder response: Typically, funders evaluate the effectiveness of the programs that their grants support at the end of a grantmaking cycle. This type of evaluation (summative evaluation) helps funders decide if and how to continue funding a particular program or organization.

More funders are conducting ongoing evaluations that begin when grantmaking programs start and continue throughout the programs' lives. The purpose of these evaluations (formative evaluations) is to inform funders of ongoing program development. These types of evaluations also provide findings to the grantees participating in the grantmaking program. This is mostly the case for a small set of larger funders who have invested a significant amount of funding into a particular initiative and have the resources to continue this type of intensive evaluation. For other funders, evaluation is something to do at the end of a grant program to make strategic decisions.

Nonprofit response: Typically, nonprofits evaluate their programs near the end of a grant in order to seek renewed funding. They do evaluate the program outputs on an ongoing basis, but analyze and report on the findings only when grant reports are due to funders. While still not the norm, some nonprofits do conduct evaluations when their organization begins a strategic planning process. Overall, nonprofits evaluate their programs when they need to prove to others that they deserve additional funding.

Partnering for learning: Funders should support (and fund) nonprofits' efforts to evaluate all of their programs on an ongoing basis. If nonprofits received more resources to strengthen their evaluation capacity, nonprofit organizations could do a better job of gathering data on how they spend their resources and on the quantity and quality of their programs and services during and at the end of every engagement with every client. Nonprofits need to build their capacity to analyze and report on the data at times when the information will be most relevant and useful for making organizational or programmatic decisions. If nonprofits were conducting evaluations on an ongoing basis, as well as using a mixed-methods design that includes some quantitative data collection methods, then funders would likely receive better reports from them. Additionally, because nonprofits would be conducting their evaluation efforts on an ongoing basis, it is likely that funder reporting requirements would not be as burdensome to the nonprofits' staff because current data would be more readily available. Ultimately, if nonprofits build their capacity to evaluate their programs using an evaluative learning approach, funders will receive much better data from their grantees. This won't replace the need for funders to conduct external evaluations of major grantmaking initiatives, but will help many small- to mid-sized funders improve what they are learning and strengthen their overall grantmaking.

How One Funder Improved Its Grantees' Evaluation Capacity

The Howard Hughes Medical Institute (HHMI) wanted to improve the evaluation capacity of its Precollege Program grantees. These biomedical research institutions, science museums, and other informal science education institutions received program funding from HHMI to implement projects to improve the science education of students (prekindergarten through grade twelve). As with many foundations, HHMI invested significant resources to evaluate its grantmaking programs to ensure program quality and the achievement of outcomes. However, HHMI began to see that conducting an evaluation of multiple grantees over many years can be costly, burdensome, and often inconclusive because of each grantee's unique context. As a result, HHMI often has difficulty generalizing evaluation findings and using them for real learning.

As such, HHMI developed a pilot Peer Evaluation Cluster Project (PECP) with the overall goal of improving each grantee's evaluation capacity. HHMI selected twelve grantees to participate in the pilot project. The project managers from these grantees were put into one of three groups of four project managers. Each group member would host a visit of their group to receive feedback on the strengths and challenges of their current evaluation methods and approaches. The site visits included observing projects and activities in action; observing evaluation data collection in action; reviewing and providing feedback on evaluation plans, tools, and instruments; and providing overall critical friendship. After each site visit, each group drafted a report for the host that highlighted strengths, challenges, and ideas identified during the site visit. The reports were shared with team members, HHMI, and other PECP groups. HHMI contracted with an outside consultant to manage, facilitate, and assess the process.

PECP proved to be a powerful peer learning experience for the participants, especially with respect to improving their evaluation plans, methods, tools, and skills. For example:

- A number of participants took suggestions made by their peers to improve survey instruments for gathering information from students or teachers.

- Some participants learned ways to use control groups where they hadn't thought it was possible.

- Participants learned to use video as an effective evaluation tool.

Most participants felt that they better understood the importance of using ongoing evaluation to continue learning and make midcourse corrections, and the importance of evaluating the "big picture" (not just the "outcomes").

All participants developed and shared their logic model with other project managers.

How Should the Evaluation Findings Be Used?

Funder response: Typically, funders use evaluation findings to make strategic grantmaking decisions. These decisions include whether to continue funding a particular program, initiative, or grantee, and if and how to increase or decrease the amount of funding for a program, initiative, or grantee. Fewer funders use evaluation findings to make ongoing changes to their program strategy. For example, some funders will use evaluation findings to provide guidance to grantees on how they should allocate the grant money. Funders may also use the evaluation findings to encourage their grantees to seek advice, guidance, or consultation when a particular programmatic or organizational problem, challenge, or barrier has been identified. However, this use of evaluation occurs less often than using the information for making decisions. Most funders use the evaluation findings for accountability to their board of trustees.

> Typically, funders use evaluation findings to make strategic grantmaking decisions. . . . Nonprofit organizations typically use evaluation findings to report to their funders that they did what they said they would do, . . . and sometimes to share the client outcomes they have achieved.

Nonprofit response: Nonprofit organizations typically use evaluation findings to report to their funders that they did what they said they would do (fully implemented their programs), and sometimes to share the client outcomes they have achieved. Nonprofits rarely use their evaluation findings to inform decision making. For example, it is uncommon for a nonprofit to share evaluation findings with board members to make policy decisions, with staff to provide feedback on performance, with financial decision makers to make resource allocation decisions, or with staff to use as a tool to increase interest for investing in the organization. These are just a few ways that nonprofits could use evaluation findings, but often don't. (Refer also to Table 1, Use of Evaluation to Improve Organizational Capacity, page 36, for ways that nonprofits could use evaluation findings to improve organizational capacity.)

Partnering for learning: If funders support and nonprofits apply an evaluative learning approach to their work, then evaluation findings can be used to revise and improve the program logic model on an ongoing basis.

With this learning, both grantmakers and grantees will have a clearer picture of how to maximize the use of resources because they will know which program elements need the most resources. If nonprofits continue to revisit and revise their logic model based on what they learn from the evaluation, the logic model will evolve from a set of *assumptions* about how programs and services achieve client outcomes to *research-based knowledge* of what it really takes to achieve client outcomes. Nonprofits will then have a set of best practice and outcome benchmarks they can use as a management tool. To date, few nonprofits have reached the point where they have program and outcome benchmarks that serve as management tools for maintaining quality program implementation, nor have they used these benchmarks to test program innovations to see if the bar can be raised. If nonprofits receive support in their evaluative learning efforts, funders will in turn benefit in the following ways:

- *Programs that funders invest in will get stronger over time.* Nonprofits and funders first need to understand what works (that is, be able to answer the question, Which program elements affect the greatest change in client outcomes?). From this understanding, nonprofits can develop a set of "best practice benchmarks" for those program elements that highly correlate with (or even cause) the desired client outcomes. Then, over time, nonprofits' efforts to improve their programs will be more effective because these benchmarks will serve as the minimum test for assessing improved success.

- *Funders will be able to make more strategic use of their finite grantmaking resources.* Funders can also learn from their grantees' evaluation findings. Funders will better understand which organizations to invest in based on the benchmark-based progress that nonprofits report, and on clearer evidence of the types of programs and services that lead to success.

- *Funders will be able to better support their grantees.* Funders will get a birds-eye view of best practices across clusters of grantees that conduct evaluative learning. This helps funders refine their grantmaking strategies and provide better guidance and support to grantees who perhaps aren't yet applying best practices that others are using as benchmarks of success.

- *Funders will be better able to prove to their boards of trustees that program grants are working and why they are working.* Evaluative learning is ongoing—therefore it increases the likelihood that the grant-supported programs will continuously improve. Boards of trustees will see a larger percent of their grant portfolio making progress. Additionally, boards of trustees will see why their grant-supported programs work, and how particular foundation-supported innovations continue to raise the bar on both the quality of programs and the client outcomes. Also, boards of trustees will have better information about grantees who fall short of benchmarks and show little progress—important information because funders' resources could go to better use.

Figure 5, Partnering for Learning, page 52, summarizes grantees' and funders' perspectives on the six questions that shape evaluation. Note the overlap in the center of the diagram that reveals the area where funders and grantees can work together to learn from and improve on the evaluation findings.

Figure 5. Partnering for Learning

	Typical Nonprofits	organizational capacity building / field building	Typical Funders
Why evaluate?	• Requirement of funding • We want to know that we make a difference	• Program and organizational planning, grantmaking	• We want to know if the grantee did what they said they'd do • We need to see if our grants are making a difference
What to evaluate?	• Quantity and quality of programs/services	• The quality and quantity of organizational resources (money and time), programs/services, and the outcome	• Quantity and quality of programs/services and outcomes
How to evaluate?	• Primarily subjective evaluation, with not so much concern for scientific rigor	• A combination of objective and subjective processes that most appropriately address program and organizational planning needs	• Objective evaluation that includes some degree of scientific rigor
Who should evaluate?	• Organizational staff and/or an internal evaluator	• Internal evaluator/staff, with an outside coach and/or evaluator if they add value to the evaluation process and organizational learning	• An outside evaluator
When to evaluate?	• At the end of the life of a program and/or at the end of an organization planning cycle	• Ongoing, in alignment with regular program and organizational planning activities	• At the end of a grantmaking program/initiative, and/or at the end of a grant cycle
How to use findings?	• To provide to funder • Reflection by organizational leaders (only)	• Sharing lessons learned with others (community and broader field)	• Making grantmaking decisions • Accountability to the board

Summary

Key points in this chapter:

- Use evaluative learning to strengthen program and organizational planning and improvement, and overall grantmaking strategies. Both funders and nonprofits will benefit.

- Evaluate the relationship between program resources (money, experience, and time), program quality, and the desired outcomes. It is critically important to the learning process to look at the big picture. Understanding how to make things better will be missing if evaluation only looks at the number of dollars spent, the number of services provided, the number of clients served, the quality of programs, or the outcomes. Individually, these elements aren't critical. What is critical to an organization's mission is if and how each of the elements works together. Evaluation is an excellent way to develop benchmarks for best practices and client outcomes.

- Be receptive to making compromises on the level of objectivity required for the evaluation, as well as the level of sophistication of the evaluation design and methods. Nonprofit organizations will not be able to conduct costly and sophisticated evaluations on an ongoing basis. However, funders will need some level of objectivity and sophistication for the purposes of accountability.

- To achieve evaluative learning, nonprofits will likely need to partner with an external evaluator, especially when an organization doesn't have the resources to hire a full-time evaluator or has a strong need for objectivity. The external evaluator should not be the sole designer and implementer of the evaluation, but rather an expert partner in the evaluative learning process.

- Evaluate on an ongoing basis, especially in alignment with regular program and organizational planning activities (both for nonprofits and funders). This may require some negotiation between the organizations so that reports and findings meet both of their planning needs.

- Funders and nonprofits can both benefit from the findings from a non-profit-driven evaluative learning process. In the long run, this type of approach to evaluation can lead specifically to identifying, using, and innovating based on benchmarks of success that prove to be beneficial to the nonprofits' organizational and programmatic planning, and the funders' strategic grantmaking decision process. However, it likely will take more time because benchmarks first need to be developed.

In this chapter, you've learned ways that funders and nonprofits can partner to learn from evaluation. The next chapter proposes specific strategies to shift current evaluation practices to evaluative learning.

Chapter Four

Step-by-Step Strategies for Supporting the Use of Evaluation as a Capacity-Building Tool

THE PREVIOUS CHAPTERS DEFINED THE EVALUATIVE learning process, presented how evaluation can be used as a capacity-building tool, and described how funders and nonprofits can partner for learning. This chapter will present the steps a funder can take to build the evaluative learning capacity of nonprofits. These steps are

Step 1: Educate your board and staff

Step 2: Assess organizational readiness

Step 3: Determine where to begin

Step 4: Assess grantees' current efforts

Step 5: Identify a set of grantees to support

Step 6: Understand strategies for supporting evaluative learning

Step 7: Set criteria, select strategies, and begin work

Step 1: Educate Your Board and Staff

Funders' boards of trustees and staff need to understand that evaluative learning can better serve their strategic grantmaking process and decisions. This book sets forth the many benefits to be gained and compromises involved. Here are some key messages to influence board and staff, organized as benefits and limitations.

Benefits of evaluative learning

- Grantee reports will have greater depth, not just reporting on outputs. Board and staff have a better chance of learning whether grants resulted in change.

- Funders will better understand whether grantees are improving over time.

- Funders will learn more about best practices—or what works. These learnings can be used to shape other grant initiatives and help other grantees improve.

- Funders can still use evaluation for accountability purposes—with some compromises (noted in the limitations listed below).

- The evaluative learning approach increases the likelihood that grantees are using evaluation findings not just for programs, but also for organizational planning and capacity building.

- Investing in grantees' evaluative learning is a cost-effective capacity-building tool. It increases the likelihood that evaluation-driven program improvements will become a long-term part of grantees' program strategies.

- Funders will better understand how they might replicate their programs, or at least critical elements of their programs.

- Funders can make more informed decisions about whether to invest in a nonprofit that they have never supported.

- Even if a funder stops funding a nonprofit, evaluative learning continues and other funders and the community continue to benefit.

- Evaluation findings will be current and relevant.

While it is important to convey these benefits to funder boards and staff, it is just as important to explain the compromises that will result from an evaluative learning approach. Because these compromises may be more difficult for funders to accept, a detailed explanation of cause follows each compromise.

Limitations of evaluative learning

• Outcome data will likely be more short-term—presenting findings on attitude, knowledge, motivation, and skill development changes.

Explanation: Most nonprofits don't have the resources or ability to track their clients postintervention, and measures of behavior change often require collecting some form of observation-based data or secondary data that is hard to gather or hard to relate directly to the intervention.

For example, measuring whether teachers apply what they learned from a professional development workshop requires an evaluator to be in the classroom. Behavior change could be measured using some form of self-report by the teacher, but tracking teachers over time requires a lot of administrative legwork and the full cooperation of teachers. Without intending to be inaccessible, teachers are, frankly, way too busy and have other priorities demanding their time and attention.

To support evaluative learning, funders will have to let go of the idea of gathering long-term behavior change data. . . . If they have the resources, they can still conduct external evaluations using evaluation and research experts to look more closely at cause and effect.

Let's say for this professional development program the nonprofit wanted to see if student achievement improved (the desired long-term outcome). The nonprofit would have to first gather students' school test score data for only the teachers who participated in the workshop. It is difficult, if not impossible, to collect secondary school-level test data that is broken out by teacher. So, let's say that the nonprofit wanted to get report card data instead. They would have to jump through a lot of hoops to gain access to report card data, including getting through school districts' internal review process designed to protect children from harm due to being research subjects. Finally, gathering data on students' academic achievement requires a working assumption that the particular professional development program for teachers was so powerful that it, and it alone, caused the academic gains—an unlikely assumption.

All of this is to say that to support evaluative learning, funders will have to let go of the idea of gathering long-term behavior change data. However, if they have the resources, they can still conduct external evaluations using evaluation and research experts to look more closely at cause and effect.

- Most likely, evaluation design will not use control or comparison groups, but rather use a simple pre- and postintervention design.

Explanation: The best design will likely be a simple pre- and posttest design where data are gathered on the desired short-term outcomes before an intervention, and then immediately following the intervention. Analyzing the data will determine if there is a significant difference between the before and after. Due to this, the findings can be generalized only to those clients receiving services, and only where outcome data are collected from all clients or a representative sample of clients. In some cases, nonprofits can't gather baseline (pre-) outcome data but only post-intervention outcome data. For example, a museum serves hundreds of people a day. They ask some guests to complete a baseline survey before entering and then come back to complete a postexperience survey. But completion rates will likely be low. With evaluative learning, however, if the museum gathers this immediate outcome data on a long-term and repeated basis, they can still use the findings to help identify the types of experiences that best enrich their guests' experience, as measured by some type of knowledge gain, attitude change, or awareness.

- While funders will get better data from their grantees than their usual reports, the quality and consistency of that data will still vary.

Explanation: Nonprofits, and particularly individuals in charge of the evaluative learning process, will not have uniform knowledge, skill, practice, or experience to conduct evaluations. As such, and especially without some outside assistance from an evaluator, the evaluation design, data collection, and findings may not be as high quality as is possible for the organization.

An Interesting Evaluation Design Conundrum

Imagine that an organization can't get enough of a sample to even generalize to its own population. For example, let's say that a zoo serving over one million people is unable to randomly sample one thousand guests, the approximate number needed to have a representative sample. It can only get three hundred guests to complete a self-report survey on conservation attitudinal and knowledge change, and the guests self-select (that is, it isn't a true random sample). A researcher would say that the zoo shouldn't generalize to its entire guest population. However, if the zoo examines its demographic and other background data that could affect the desired outcome for the three hundred guests, and finds that the respondents proportionally represent what the zoo knows about its overall population, the zoo can still use the data to begin understanding of the effects of its programs.

To be sure, the zoo should not present these data to the community and others in the field without clearly stating the design flaws and lack of generalizability. And the zoo should review past and current research and other related evaluations to see if what it learned seems in line with what others found. *The point is that the findings still provide a better picture of what is working than if the zoo didn't gather the data at all.* Additionally, because the zoo is using evaluative learning, and it continues to gather data on a regular basis, it will be better able to determine if a pattern persists in terms of outcomes. From this repeated process, the zoo can gain confidence in the findings that remain the same as when it first collected data. Evaluative learning helps to ameliorate some of the limitations in the necessary and practical research design that nonprofits can use because data are continuously being collected and analyzed.

- Grantees will need both financial support and technical assistance.

Explanation: Implementing an evaluative learning process has a cost. Most nonprofits will need resources to pay for staff time to conduct evaluative learning processes—to train staff or to hire an evaluator to provide technical assistance, guidance, or coaching. Funders too often ask their grantees to conduct evaluations without providing the support grantees need to do so.

Imagine you, the funder, are not a philanthropic institution but a business investor. An entrepreneur approaches you and shares with you his or her idea for a new widget, convinces you that it will make money, and asks for financial backing. Would you, as the investor, say that you will financially back the entrepreneur by providing money for *only* his or her product and the machine and staff needed to produce the product? Wouldn't a smart investor want to provide the necessary money to ensure that product development, testing, and production, as well as management, marketing, space, facilities, machines, and financial management are all in place and effective? By limiting the use of the money to production only, the investor either has to hope other investors will support the company infrastructure or to know that their investment will surely fail.

In the philanthropic sector, it is rare for another funder (investor) to support the organizational infrastructure. With respect to evaluative learning, this means an investment in product development, testing, production, and quality control. The only true test a company has for knowing if its product development, testing, production, and quality control are effective is by measuring the outcome on an ongoing basis—measuring revenues and profit. This is evaluative learning.

Step 2: Assess Organizational Readiness

Once you have educated your board of trustees and staff, it is important to assess their "readiness" to support evaluative learning. This step's goal is to determine your foundation's potential level of commitment to support evaluative learning.

Three levels of readiness are important to consider. These levels include attitudes, beliefs, or attributes that, if present, indicate the organization's decision makers are ready to shift to evaluative learning. The levels are divided as

A. *Absolutely necessary.* These are prerequisites; if the organization doesn't have these in some form, evaluative learning is not likely until the attributes are nurtured.

B. *Very important.* These attributes should be present among the majority of the organization's decision makers.

C. *Important.* These are helpful but not essential attributes.

The more characteristics the decision makers have, the better the chances of changing evaluation practices.

Absolutely necessary attributes

Funders need to have the following attributes if they are to consider providing support for evaluative learning.

- *A history or willingness to provide capacity-building grants.* At minimum, a funder should be willing to provide support for capacity building. For some funders, this may mean that program staff have some flexibility for allocating nonprogram funding to current program grantees. Others may provide additional grant dollars to program grants that a nonprofit can use for capacity building. Some funders have shown this history and willingness by providing operating support.

- *An overall belief that evaluation is about more than accountability.* As this book points out, evaluative learning is not solely about accountability. If the key decision makers at a philanthropic institution (for example, program directors, the executive director, or board members) don't believe in the need for evaluating and understanding anything other than client outcomes, then evaluative learning will not likely be supported.

- *Resources or access to resources for grantees to improve their capacity for evaluative learning.* Nonprofits need financial resources to really institutionalize evaluative learning. Funders that can't offer financial support can offer nonmonetary support like (a) referrals to technical assistance providers or management support organizations that are subsidized by the funder or other funders, (b) connections with funders that might support the work with a grant, or (c) information about low-cost or fully subsidized trainings, workshops, and so forth. If a funder can at least provide access to resources, then it can support evaluative learning.

- *Patience.* It takes time for nonprofits that are not conducting evaluation to develop the systems and capacity to conduct evaluative learning processes. They will need time to develop a plan and, if they can't get the necessary resources all at once, the process will have to happen in small steps. Funders will not see the most beneficial kinds of evaluation findings from these nonprofits in the same kind of time frame as if they hired an external evaluator to evaluate a grantee or grantmaking program.

Very important attributes

Most key decision makers need to have all of the following attributes to support evaluative learning.

- *A belief that evaluation is critical to determining whether the funder is achieving its mission.* If most key decision makers don't believe that evaluation is critical for judging whether a funder is achieving its mission, they won't likely support evaluative learning.

- *A belief that evaluation should be used to improve grantmaking.* This belief is evident when program staff themselves evaluate their grantees beyond just what's on paper through efforts like site visits. If program evaluation isn't used to make grantmaking decisions, evaluative learning may not be viewed as important or used most effectively (from the funder's perspective).

- *A belief that evaluation should benefit both funders and grantees.* Many funders conduct evaluations of grantees that don't get shared with the grantees. They also conduct little discussion about the findings in terms of implications for the grant and how the grantee could show improvement. This reflects a view that evaluation is not really beneficial to the grantee. As a part of this "readiness factor," funders need to be more transparent with their grantees as to the funders' decision-making process, regardless of the ultimate decision. This feedback is important for grantees to hear, good or bad.

- *A belief that evaluation can improve a nonprofit's organizational effectiveness in addition to its program effectiveness.* Besides improving program design and planning, evaluative learning provides invaluable information for organizational planning and decision making, as well as helps to identify where other forms of capacity building could prove useful. If funders know of this particular use of evaluative learning, but don't believe it can serve this function, then they may not view evaluative learning as important.

- *A belief that without evaluation, the opportunity to understand whether and how a nonprofit is achieving its mission is lost.* Without evaluating client outcomes, program strategies, and the resources necessary for high-quality program implementation, there is really no way to know whether nonprofits are achieving success in relation to their mission. Funders need to believe that evaluating the whole logic model is critical not only for assessing whether the mission is being accomplished (client outcomes are being realized), but also why and how. Nonprofits can achieve their mission only through understanding the why and how; the outcomes only tell them whether they have achieved their mission.

- *A long-term commitment to some or all grantees, if they are showing mission progress.* Nonprofits often have to significantly change or even eliminate programs when they lose funding. If these organizations conduct evaluative learning processes to determine what works and doesn't work, the learning stops when programs are eliminated. If nonprofits manage to acquire funding elsewhere to continue programs, they will be able to continue their evaluative learning but will likely have to make some (hopefully minor) changes to their design, data collection tools, and how they report findings. By helping to build the evaluative learning capacity of nonprofits, original funders help ensure that the approach continues. However, changes will have to be made, and will involve some additional cost in time and perhaps money for nonprofits.

Important attributes

Funders need to have, or develop, the following attributes to commit to evaluative learning.

- *A history of using evaluation for funder and grantee learning.* Funders who have experience evaluating their individual grants or grantmaking programs, especially in conducting evaluations where grantees were involved throughout the process, have experienced the benefits to themselves and their grantees firsthand. As a result, they are more likely to commit to supporting evaluative learning.

- *Strong relationships and frequent communication with some or all grantees.* Funders who meet with their grantees frequently through activities like site visits, and who have formed the types of relationships with their grantees where nonprofits feel safe discussing challenges, delays, or problems, are in a good position to engage these grantees in evaluative learning.

- *A clear logic model or program model for grantmaking initiatives.* Funders who have spent time articulating their grantmaking program's logic model will have a clear sense of the types of outcomes they seek to achieve, and by when; the specific strategies that will achieve the outcomes; and the resources grantees will need to implement the strategies. By going through the process of developing their own logic model, funders are better able to communicate their evaluation needs to their grantees, as well as ensure that their grantees' logic models are similar. As a result, when grantees move forward with an evaluative learning process, they are better able to design their evaluation with both the funder's learning needs and their own learning needs in mind.

- *Access to evaluation technical assistance providers or evaluators for grantees.* Nonprofits often don't know whom to turn to for evaluation assistance. Funders, due to engaging evaluators; providing grants to nonprofits to hire evaluators; or having access to the local, regional, or national network of funders and technical assistance providers, can serve as effective brokers for bringing nonprofits together with evaluators who can become an expert partner in the evaluative learning process.

Appendix A includes a "Funder Readiness Tool" that can help you and your organization determine its level of readiness for evaluative learning.

Step 3: Determine Where to Begin

Most funders will not likely be in the position to invest resources (money, time, networks, and information) toward supporting evaluative learning for all of their grantees. As such, it is important that funders take the time to make deliberate decisions about how to spend their resources so they get the kinds of information that will improve their grantmaking and ultimately achieve their mission. Funders will need to match their own learning needs with their grantees so the grantees can also make best use of an evaluative learning process. Two tasks will help your foundation get ready to support evaluative learning:

A. Assess the current grant portfolio to select a program or outcome focus for supporting evaluative learning

B. Develop a logic model for the program area of interest

Assess the current grant portfolio to select a program or outcome focus for supporting evaluative learning

Funders need to identify the desired outcomes and strategies to focus their support of evaluative learning on. Consider the following questions:

- *What program strategy and outcomes do funders want to learn the most about?* The answer to this question will depend on the following factors:

  - The amount of funding committed to a particular program strategy or outcome—if the amount of funding is high, funders may want to focus their support in this area.

  - The size of "per-grantee" investments—if funders provide large grants to a small number of nonprofits, then this might be where they want to focus.

  - The number of key internal decision makers interested in the particular strategy or outcomes—this will ensure buy-in to the process.

  - Whether the strategy or outcomes play a significant role in reducing a community problem or fill a gap in needed services—evaluative learning would allow funders to obtain more information about their role in ameliorating this problem.

  - Whether the learning that could come from this approach to evaluation will help advance the field.

- *What grantmaking programs or initiatives do funders want to improve?* Perhaps a particular initiative has stalled or needs some additional non-programmatic support to more effectively achieve its desired outcomes.

When funders provide support under this program umbrella, grantees' improved learning will benefit funders by helping to identify (a) program strengths and weaknesses, (b) resource issues that may not be addressed, and (c) organizational capacity challenges that grantees may be encountering that, with some additional capacity building, could be removed.

- *Can evaluative learning help funders to understand why a certain set of grantees seems particularly innovative and effective?* Funders should look at their grant portfolio and determine if there is great work going on that should be continued and sustained or better understood so others can benefit. Sometimes investing to improve effective nonprofits' evaluative capacity can go a long way toward helping those same nonprofits sustain their work because they will develop better benchmarks of success (identify best practices), allowing them to continue the work and even innovate for improvement. Additionally, nonprofits and funders can both benefit from the learning by disseminating the knowledge of what works to others. Finally, when effective organizations can measure and present how their programs achieve the desired outcomes, funders will have better indicators for determining and supporting other nonprofits that are striving for the same outcomes.

Once funders take time to prioritize and answer these questions, they will be better able to decide where to invest evaluative learning resources.

Develop a logic model for the program area of interest

Hopefully, by completing the previous task, funders have narrowed down where they want to begin investing in evaluative learning to a particular set of related outcomes and the strategies that will achieve these outcomes. And funders will likely have a better sense of the pool of grantees they are looking at. The next task is to develop a logic model for the program area of interest. (Refer to Appendix B, Logic Model Development Tool, for a tool that will help funders develop a logic model.)

Great resources exist for developing a logic model. Two worth looking into are the W. K. Kellogg Foundation's Logic Model Development Guide[xiii] and Innovation Network's Logic Model Builder™, a web-based tool that can be accessed at www.innonet.org. Both of these tools can help a funder generate a logic model for a program area or initiative.

One recommendation for developing a logic model is to involve as many stakeholders (people who will be affected by the process or findings) as possible in the process. For funders this could involve board members, the executive director, program staff, other staff, and, ideally, grantee representatives.

Hiring someone to help facilitate the logic model development process may be beneficial in some cases. The logic model process is grounded in the principle that everyone comes together to discuss their assumptions about the outcomes that should be accomplished, the strategies that are needed to achieve the outcomes, and the resources needed to support the strategies. While this may sound simple, it often requires a lot of discussion to agree on the overall model. An outside facilitator can help this process by serving as a resource for getting clarification where there is confusion or disagreement, making sure the process doesn't get stalled, and pulling it all together for the stakeholders.

Finally, the logic model process must not stop at just identifying the outcomes, strategies, and resources. It should always include the "arrows" that interconnect these components. One of the central points of this book is that evaluative learning happens most when we understand which strategies affect the desired outcome and which inputs best support the strategies that work. Therefore, funders and nonprofits alike need to specify their assumptions about these relationships.

By developing a logic model for the funders' program areas of interest, funders will be better able to (a) communicate their learning needs with their grantees, (b) engage in a discussion as to how their logic model over-laps with grantees' program logic model and where it does not, and (c) ensure that any evaluative learning process that funders support meets their grantees' learning needs.

With a clear set of program strategies and outcomes to focus on and a fully articulated logic model, funders are ready to move to the next step—assessing what types of evaluation and evaluative learning are already happening.

Step 4: Assess Grantees' Current Efforts

Before moving ahead, funders need to know and understand what types of evaluation and evaluative learning processes are available to and already going on among their grantees. Grantees may already be evaluating their work, including using available technical assistance. Other funders could have invested resources into evaluating the grantees' programs. By first examining what's going on, a funder won't duplicate efforts, and in fact could leverage those opportunities to improve the use of evaluative learning. Let's take a closer look at helping your foundation to assess what's going on, captured via two tasks:

A. Talk to the grantees

B. Talk to other funders

Talk to the grantees

Now that funders have identified a particular set of strategies and outcomes they want to focus on along with a pool of grantees who are working on these strategies and outcomes, and have developed their logic model, they need to talk with these grantees about the grantees' current evaluation efforts. If there are too many grantees to talk to, funders will want to select a representative sample from the pool of grantees. The following set of questions, which in large part are the same questions addressed in Chapter 3 in the "partnering for learning" sections, need to be answered through this interaction:

- *Is your organization currently implementing any evaluation efforts?*

- *If so, why is your organization conducting these evaluation efforts?* Funders should try to assess to what degree their grantees are conducting evaluation efforts for accountability and to whom. Funders should also assess how the grantees are using evaluation to inform both program planning and organizational planning.

- *What is your organization evaluating?* Specifically, funders want to learn if their grantees are evaluating outcomes, strategies, inputs, or relationships among these components.

- *How is your organization evaluating its programs?* Funders want to learn about the evaluation design. Specifically, funders want to learn about data collection methodologies (comparison groups, pre-intervention and post-intervention, post-only, client satisfaction surveys, tracking or logging of services rendered or other outputs, surveys about the quality of services or programs), as well as data collection tools (surveys, focus groups, structured interviews, secondary data collection, documentation).

- *Who is involved in designing and implementing your evaluation efforts?* Funders should determine who within the grantee's organization is designing the evaluation efforts, helping with data collection and analysis, and helping to present findings. Funders need to also determine if an outside evaluator is involved and what their role is in the design, data collection and analysis, and reporting.

- *When does your organization conduct its evaluation efforts?* Specifically, when do grantees gather data on
  - The resources used (for example, the time staff spend with clients, information provided to clients)

– The quantity of service delivery (for example, number of clients served, number of services provided per client)

– The quality of services (for example, client satisfaction with services, client ratings of program elements that the grantee identified as critical to client success, alignment between client ratings of services and what is known about best practices)

– Short-term outcomes (for example, attitude changes, knowledge gains, skill development, motivation change)

– Long-term outcomes (for example, behavioral improvements, performance improvements, system changes)

• *How does your organization use evaluation findings?* Funders want to understand if grantees use evaluations for the following:

– Program planning

– Organizational planning, including strategic planning

– Governance decisions

– Human resource management

– Fundraising

– Financial management

– Marketing

– Community outreach, including collaborating and forming strategic alliances with other nonprofits

– Disseminating information to community constituents

– Disseminating information to the field (that is, similar organizations or networks, affiliate groups, associations in the region or country)

– Other uses

This will help funders understand if and how grantees are using evaluation as a capacity-building tool.

- *How much time and money does your organization currently allocate toward evaluation?* Funders need to understand how much staff time and organizational funding grantees allocate toward evaluation efforts.

- *If your organization uses outside help, like an evaluation consultant, are you satisfied with their assistance?* Funders will want to know more about if and how their grantees seek and use evaluation assistance, and if their learning needs are met. A key question for funders to ask is whether the consultant or technical assistance provider has provided advice, guidance, or actual evaluation services, as well as built the organization's capacity to conduct evaluation on an ongoing basis. If this is the case, funders will want to know who is providing the assistance because this evaluator could serve as a resource for other grantees.

- *If you are conducting evaluations for other funders, who are these funders, and what are they asking for?* In most cases nonprofits have multiple funders, many of whom request evaluation findings. It is important for funders to understand what other funders require of their grantees, especially with respect to information about resources, the quantity and quality of strategies, and outcomes. It is a good idea to request reporting templates from these other funders, with permission of course.

This brings us to the next task necessary for assessing what's going on.

Talk to other funders

Once funders have a clearer picture of what their grantees are doing with respect to evaluation (especially the grantees that are a part of the pool of grantees representing the *funder's* desired program or outcome focus), they should talk to these grantees' other funders. It is likely that this list of funders is small. The goal of talking with these funders is to answer the following questions:

- *What are the common strategies and outcomes that both funders are working on?* The point of this question is to determine if the program or outcome focus that the funder interested in supporting evaluative learning

(Funder A) is shared with the other funder (Funder B). This becomes the starting place for the next questions.

• *What evaluation requirements does Funder B have of their grantees (those grantees in common), and how, if at all, does Funder B support the grantee to meet these requirements?* Funder A needs to learn from Funder B what it requires of its grantees with respect to evaluation. Funder A will also want to know, if it doesn't come up, how much money and other resources Funder B provides to its grantees for these evaluation efforts.

• *Does or would Funder B support improving the use of evaluation as a capacity-building tool?* In large part, the prior question will help to answer this question. However, it would be good to have a conversation to determine whether Funder B ascribes to the philosophy of using evaluation as a capacity-building tool. If it doesn't, then Funder A needs to be aware that its grantee will have to meet both funders' needs, and the needs may be different. This helps Funder A develop more appropriate and feasible strategies for supporting its grantees' evaluative learning, whether or not Funder B also supports evaluative learning.

• *Would Funder B consider pooling resources to improve a set of common grantees' abilities to develop its capacity for evaluative learning?* By asking this question, local funders can begin to think about and develop joint strategies for supporting evaluative learning. In this way they can share the cost while at the same time jointly benefit from the learning that occurs for the grantees they commonly support. Additionally, and most important, this will likely lead to a decrease in the ever-growing burden that grantees face to be accountable to their funders—each of whom is likely to have different program evaluation or reporting requirements.

• *Does Funder B know of local evaluation consultants or technical assistance providers (like management support organizations) who would be a good resource for grantees' evaluative learning efforts?* Asking this question of funders, as well as grantees (refer above), allows Funder A to develop a list of appropriate evaluation providers and services for supporting its grantees.

Step 5: Identify a Set of Grantees to Support

Now that you have gathered information on how and why your grantees are conducting evaluation, what other funders are asking of the grantees, and the ways in which you and other funders might come together to support evaluative learning, you are ready to identify a set of grantees to support. The following questions will help you determine grantees' readiness. (The questionnaire in Appendix C, Assessing Grantees' Readiness for Evaluative Learning, can be used to help assess grantee readiness).

- *Does the organization have strong leaders?* Strong organizational leadership is needed if evaluative learning is to be valued and institutionalized. Strong leaders and board members (because they play a key leadership role for an organization) need to value learning, including having the information, tools, and full staff input that support an organizational learning process. Evaluative learning will not be institutionalized without board buy-in.

- *Is there some measurable and objective evidence of current organizational learning?* Measurable evidence should include documents, reports, databases, technology systems, as well as written staff job descriptions, plans, and other policies and procedures that indicate the organization does or has most of the following:
  - Organizational assessments
  - Client needs assessments
  - Environmental scans (examining opportunities and threats)
  - Program evaluation
  - Knowledge
  - Networking
  - Collaborating
  - Research

Additionally, some documentation or report should show that the grant-ee has spent organizational resources (money and time) conducting the efforts. However, little to no evidence of these things doesn't mean that evaluative learning shouldn't be supported. Rather, it means that more time and resources may be needed to build their capacity. Because many funders want to begin small with respect to supporting evaluative learn-ing, it may be better to first improve the evaluative capacity of those grantees who have some capacity for organizational learning.

- *How receptive will staff be to conducting evaluative learning?* Many non-profit professionals have felt threatened, burdened, and perhaps even punished due to prior evaluation efforts. And most individuals do not like to feel that they are being graded. As such, while evaluative learn-ing is a tool for helping organizations identify human resource strengths and challenges, staff will need to feel they are learning from the process rather than being judged or punished by it. More specifically, staff will need to know that the evaluative learning process will identify, build on, and support strengths for addressing any challenges. Staff will be more receptive if they already feel their managers and organizational leaders have approached them from a strength-based approach to problem solv-ing. This is difficult to assess, but critically important. Evaluative learning shouldn't be used as a tool or even an excuse for organizational leaders to make hiring or firing decisions. Staff turnover can be one indication of staff readiness; however, funders will need to look closely at the cause of that turnover before prejudging it to be a reflection of weakness-based management practices.

Once you have identified a set of grantees that seem ready to move forward on their evaluative learning efforts, you need to determine the best strate-gies for supporting evaluative learning. But before you can do that, you'll need an understanding of the basic strategies available to you, the topic of Step 6.

Step 6: Understand Strategies for Supporting Evaluative Learning

This step entails determining the best approach for supporting grantees' evaluative capacity-building efforts considering

A. The funders' current investment resources

B. Investments that would support what nonprofits are already doing

C. The nonprofits' readiness to improve their evaluative learning

All of the steps thus far should have led you to understand what your needs and your grantees' needs are, what other funders are doing to support evaluation and evaluative learning, and how much to invest in this effort. What follows is a presentation of a number of strategies that funders can support,

---

Strategies at a Glance

Low-cost strategies

- Ensure that your mission, vision, goals, and objectives fit with those of the grantee
- Assess the fit between your logic model and the grantee's logic model
- Align evaluation requirements of multiple funders for a single grantee
- Request clear evaluation designs from grantees

Medium-cost strategies

- Change how evaluation information is requested from grantees
- Provide funding or referrals to local evaluation providers

- Sponsor evaluation workshops for some or all grantees
- Supply an evaluation coach to grantees

High-cost strategies

- Provide professional development for grantees' internal evaluators
- Fund peer-to-peer exchanges (peer site visits and meetings)
- Fund an external evaluator to assess one or more of your grantmaking programs
- Fund grantees to hire outside evaluators
- Fund the development of grantee evaluation plans and systems

---

in order from least costly to most costly (in terms of both money and time for both funders and grantees).

Note to the reader: Refer to Table 2, Evaluative Learning Support Strategies, page 95, to view a summary of the following evaluative learning support strategies, ranked from highest to lowest capacity-building potential.

Low-cost strategies

The following strategies represent a change in the way funders currently interact with their grantees about evaluation. These steps don't help nonprofits greatly improve their evaluative learning, but they are sometimes the first steps that funders can take, especially smaller funders.

- **Ensure that the funders' mission, vision, goals, and objectives fit with those of grantees.** Funders need to look at their overall institutional and grantmaking program mission, vision, goals, and objectives to ensure that potential grantees share a similar or related mission, vision, goals, and objectives. For example, let's say a funder is supporting programs with the mission of eliminating homelessness. A nonprofit organization that provides job training to underemployed (but housed) individuals applies and receives funding that supports its programs because the nonprofit makes the argument that it is "preventing" homelessness. The funder hasn't ever funded job training programs. It is the funder's choice to make this grant, and perhaps it is a rational choice. However, because the nonprofit's mission is to improve the employment picture for their clients, and not decrease homelessness, they are currently not measuring any outcomes related to homelessness. When the funder requests evaluation data, particularly outcome data from this grantee, they will likely ask for measures of outcomes related to homelessness. One of two things will happen: the funder will ask for these types of measures, so the grantee will be burdened with evaluating an outcome that doesn't relate to their mission, or the funder won't ask for measures of decreases in homelessness and will therefore not get adequate findings that help them assess their own mission.

Cost to the funder: low. This should already be a part of the grantmaking process.

Cost to the grantee: low. They may spend a little time providing information to the funder; however, this information was likely already a part of their proposal.

Capacity-building potential: medium. The grantee really doesn't learn much from this, but hopefully the funder makes better decisions making it more likely that the nonprofit will employ evaluative learning processes because they won't be asked to evaluate something unrelated to their mission.

- **Assess the fit between the funder's and grantee's logic models.** When both the funder and grantee have developed logic models, they will be much more likely to determine strategies and outcomes they both have in common. If there is nothing in common, then one wonders why the funder is supporting the grantee. Shared strategies and outcomes provide funders and grantees a beginning point to explore where to focus the grantee's evaluative learning efforts.

  Cost to the funder: low. The funder will need time, knowledge, and experience to develop the logic model.

  Cost to the grantee: low. The grantee will need time, knowledge, and experience to develop a logic model.

  Capacity-building potential: medium. The grantee and funder can both learn from the logic model process. More specifically, they can articulate their assumptions for how their programs will achieve the desired outcomes. The logic model development and dissemination process helps set the stage for further evaluative learning strategies.

- **Align evaluation requirements with what other funders require of the grantees.** It is likely that through the previous steps of talking with grantees and other funders, an organization has learned about the evaluation efforts of their grantees, as well as what the grantees' other funders require. Using this information, the funder should try to gather findings that the grantee is already measuring and ask them to develop new evaluation methods and measures for only those strategies and outcomes that they are not currently assessing. Funders should ask only for evaluation data they need to assess their own grantmaking programs.

Cost to the funder: low. Requires only that funders spend the time to gather information from their grantees and the grantees' other funders as to what is being evaluated.

Cost to the grantee: low. Requires only that grantees spend time providing their funders with information about the grantees' current evaluation efforts.

Capacity building potential: medium. This strategy conveys to the grantees that the funders are flexible. It goes a long way toward building the kind of funder-nonprofit relationship that, in the long run, will set the stage for improving the evaluative learning process.

- **Request clear evaluation designs from grantees.** Requesting an evaluation design, including information about *how* grantees intend to use the evaluation process and findings allows funders to gauge whether grantees are maximizing their evaluative learning, as well as the match between the funders' and grantees' learning needs. Asking for the design and specifically how the evaluation is going to be used to inform program development and organizational planning allows grantees to understand the value that funders place on grantees' learning. This request also encourages grantees to begin thinking about ways to improve evaluation efforts to maximize learning. However, making this request without some additional support could burden grantees who don't have the resources to meet the request.

Cost to the funder: low. Requires only that funders spend the time making the request and answering any questions grantees may have.

Cost to the grantee: medium. Grantees will need to spend time designing their evaluation and may need to engage an evaluation technical assistance provider.

Capacity-building potential: low. By designing an evaluation and identifying how they will use the findings, grantees are taking a first, critical step to prepare to fully implement evaluative learning. However, implementation will require a much larger investment of time and staff.

Medium-cost strategies

These medium-cost strategies are feasible for many funders and can make a more significant change in the use of evaluative learning.

- **Change how evaluation information is requested from grantees.** One way funders can improve evaluative learning—that will cost more in time, but not money—is to change the way they ask for evaluation findings from their grantees (that is, change their reporting requirements). For example, funders could begin supporting evaluative learning by asking a few key questions of their grantees through their grant closeout reports.

  - What did you evaluate?

  - How did you evaluate?

  - What did you learn about your programs through these evaluation efforts?

  - What did you learn about your organization, and what changes in your programs or organization did you make as a result?

The last three questions are evaluative learning questions and provide grantees the opportunity to share how they are learning and how they used that learning to make improvements. Funders in turn get information about their grantees' learning and change process, which may be more indicative of a strong organization than just the outputs or the results (outcomes). Through this simple set of questions, funders can communicate the value they place on learning, especially through evaluation, and grantees can spend time reflecting on their learning process, perhaps in a way they hadn't been asked to before.

Cost to the funder: medium. Requires time to revise the reporting tool and to review the findings.

Cost to the grantee: medium. Requires additional time to reflect and report on how they use their evaluation findings to improve programs and their organizations.

Capacity-building potential: medium to high. Grantees spend time reflecting on how they did or could use their evaluation effort as a learning tool.

- **Provide funding or referrals to local evaluation providers.** Management support organizations, nonprofit technical assistance providers, and consultants can serve as resources to grantees. In Step 4, funders spoke with both their grantees and other funders to identify local evaluation resources (management support organizations, technical assistance providers, consultants). Informing grantees about these resources can significantly help them obtain the kinds of assistance they need. Funders can also provide a grant to a local management support organization or technical assistance provider to help one or more of their grantees develop their evaluative learning approach and system.

It is important to note that not all evaluators have the training or skills to help nonprofits build their capacity to conduct evaluative learning. Many evaluators are wedded to social science research methodologies and, as a result, have difficulty engaging with and allowing nonprofit organizations to make decisions about the evaluation design, methodologies, tools, data collection processes, analysis, and understanding of the findings. Additionally, many evaluators are trained as researchers and have little training in facilitating organizational development. In fact, in a 2002 article, Marty Campbell and Charles McClintock point out that "there are few evaluators who possess both the research and OD [organizational development] skills necessary to make evaluation useful for program improvement." [xiv]

As a solution, the James Irvine Foundation recently partnered with the Fielding Graduate Institute to offer training to evaluators to develop their organizational development skills. While this is encouraging, funders will still face barriers to identifying evaluation providers who can also provide assistance going beyond the findings to help facilitate organizational and programmatic change. Thus, funders' support of further professional development of evaluators will be an indirect benefit to achieving the desired evaluative learning goals of their grantees. For communities having few evaluation providers who currently use an evaluative learning approach or many traditional research-based evaluators, it is important for funders to educate evaluators as to the evaluative learning process, and identify those evaluators whose philosophy is in line with evaluative learning. A good starting place is to identify organizational development specialists who also have evaluation training and experience.

Cost to the funder: medium to low. If a community has good evaluative learning resources, funders will have to spend little time helping their grantees identify these sources of assistance. To invest in the organizational development of management support organizations, technical assistance providers, or consultants will require some investment of money. To further develop the professional development skills of evaluators will also likely require some type of financial investment.

Cost to the grantee: none.

Capacity-building potential: medium to high. With more local resources available—especially for evaluative learning assistance—grantees in a given community can begin to use them and, indirectly, improve their programs and organizations.

- **Sponsor evaluation workshops for some or all grantees.** Many grantees are not aware of how evaluation can be used as a critical capacity-building tool, even beyond program development. As such, funders could sponsor a number of workshops, ranging from providing an overview of evaluative learning to developing the full spectrum of evaluative learning skills including evaluation design, the use of logic models, data collection tool development, sampling, data collection and analysis, and reporting.

  The difference between "evaluative learning" workshops and "evaluation" workshops is that while both should help to develop evaluation and research skills, evaluative learning workshops should ground what is taught in the principles of evaluative learning: ongoing, stakeholder led, collaboratively designed, and based in a logic model framework. In addition to teaching evaluation skills, these workshops should also instruct participants on how to institutionalize the learning process, use the findings for both program and organizational development, partner with funders, and develop benchmarks of success that can be used as a management and leadership tool. In addition to some core evaluation skill development, leaders of grantees need to understand how to leverage their evaluation efforts to maximize programmatic and organizational learning.

Cost to the funder: medium. Costs include paying for a workshop presenter's time, designing a workshop (if one doesn't already exist), and paying for space, facilities, materials, and food (logistical and setting costs). Funders will also have to spend time identifying capacity builders who can facilitate an evaluative learning workshop. In many communities this may not be easy, in which case funders should make it a priority to first develop the capacity of the local capacity builders. Workshops are not a long-term investment. If high-quality training is used in combination with other low-cost strategies, grantees will begin to develop their evaluative learning processes.

Cost to the grantee: medium. Grantees will have to spend time and perhaps some money to participate in a workshop. After the workshop, grantees will need more time to actually begin implementing what they learned. If funders institute some of the low-cost strategies, grantees will have some incentive to apply what they have learned.

Capacity-building potential: high. This is especially the case if used in conjunction with other funder-supported evaluative learning strategies. Note, however, that workshops as a capacity-building tool are not particularly effective on their own. Participants often need incentives or support to apply what is learned. To maximize a workshop's benefit, organizational change agents should participate because they are more likely to hold the power needed to make organizational changes. Additionally, having more than one staff member from an organization attend the workshop allows him or her to serve as an additional source for educating others in the organization and providing support to other attendees.

- **Provide an evaluation coach to some or all grantees.** An evaluation coach should be someone with evaluation and organizational development experience who can provide a pool of time for a grantee who is building their evaluative learning approach and systems to tap into when needed. Coaches should not to do the work of the evaluation, but should provide support and guidance to ensure that the goals and objectives of the evaluative learning process are met. If barriers or challenges exist within the organization or with respect to evaluation design, tools, methods, analysis, or report generation, coaches can use both their organizational and evaluation expertise and experience to help an organization get unstuck. Coaches will likely not be needed on a permanent basis, but rather just during the early stages of developing an evaluative learning system. Once the system has been institutionalized, much less—or none—of their time will be needed.

Cost to the funder: medium. The cost of using an evaluation coach is based on their daily rate and how many hours per month that funders want to support, and more important, that grantees need.

Cost to the grantee: medium. Grantees' most significant cost is time spent preparing for, participating in, and following up on coaching sessions. They will also likely have to spend time identifying the best coach to meet their organizational and programmatic learning needs, as well as their needs for evaluation technical assistance.

Capacity-building potential: high. However, coaching will only work for organizations that are ready for evaluative learning, have a clear plan for developing an evaluation system, and have a clear evaluation design. The coach is really there to support organizational leaders' efforts to take evaluative learning to the next level. More specifically, the coach is there to help organizations maximize their evaluation efforts for the purposes of decision making and capacity building.

High-cost strategies

The following high-cost strategies will likely have the greatest impact on evaluative learning for both funders and grantees. However, the evaluation provider field has a long way to go before funders all over the country can capitalize on these strategies because the strategies require evaluators to have two sets of knowledge, experience, and skills that many don't possess: (1) organizational development—a working understanding of organizational effectiveness and functions, and the organizational development consulting experience and skills that evaluators need to help facilitate the learning process through the use of evaluation tools and methods; and (2) an understanding or belief in the evaluative learning approach, including an understanding and appreciation for the research design compromises that will likely be needed to maximize organizational learning. Nonetheless, funders can implement the following high-cost strategies.

- **Provide professional development for grantees' internal evaluators.** Funders can provide the resources necessary for their grantees who use an internal evaluator to receive more intensive training on how to use evaluation as a capacity-building tool. This training needs to incorporate three things: (1) core evaluation or research skill development, where needed; (2) organizational development skills that provide evaluators with an understanding of organizational effectiveness and functions so that they can help leaders make maximum use of the findings for all capacity building; and (3) strategies for synthesizing and reporting findings that increase their usability. The assumption is that grantees receiving this kind of support are large enough to have a part-time or full-time evaluator and are ready to implement an evaluative learning approach.

  Cost to the funder: medium to high. Supporting this strategy will require a financial investment in training that is more than a workshop. Three separate trainings may be needed: evaluation, organizational development, and evaluative learning or organizational learning.

  Cost to the grantee: medium. Grantees will have to spend time and money to participate in the training. Afterwards, they will likely need to invest time and money into improving the systems or technology needed to support the increased application of evaluative learning principles.

  Capacity-building potential: high. Grantees who already have an internal evaluator likely have already recognized the value of evaluation beyond accountability. However, with additional training the internal evaluator can improve grantees' current evaluation methods, tools, and systems to maximize organizational learning.

- **Provide funding for peer exchange.** Existing evidence shows that a structured, facilitated, ongoing, and participant-led peer exchange process can serve as an effective capacity-building tool for developing many of the core capacities that grantees need to succeed. Peer exchange, for example, has been used and proven to be an effective leadership development capacity-building tool. But, can peer exchange improve the skills necessary for improving adaptive capacities like evaluation, client needs assessment, and organizational assessment? These activities require a certain level of technical expertise.

It is clear that peer mentoring can help grantees' adaptive capacity by increasing their networks and collaborative activities. But it isn't clear whether peer mentoring can serve to develop the evaluation skills necessary for evaluative learning. Interestingly, the Howard Hughes Medical Institute (HHMI) recently tested a peer exchange approach to improving the evaluation capacity of their grantees. The sidebar, How One Funder Improved Its Grantees' Evaluation Capacity, on page 48, notes how this process has in fact led to improvements in participating organizations' evaluation capacity, and specifically their use of evaluation as a capacity-building tool. Participants have improved data collection tools; shared data collection tools; provided feedback and modifications on evaluation design, including the use of control or comparison groups; and provided needed peer-based and therefore nonthreatening support and guidance.

Principally two elements can make up a peer exchange process, and both in conjunction increase the learning significantly:

– Conduct site visits: Groups of three to four peers (change agents within their organization) conduct site visits with one another, spending a few days discussing the host's evaluation needs and efforts, and providing feedback and other resources that could prove useful. Grantees are more likely to feel secure with the site visit process if they are not in the same community because they do not perceive each other as competitors. However, site visits can work in the same community once relationships and trust have been built among a group of peers. To build trust, consider first supporting the next peer exchange process.

– Conduct regular and ongoing meetings of peers: Groups of six to eight grantees (again, change agents in their organizations) meet monthly for at least two hours to discuss their evaluation and evaluative learning efforts, get feedback, and share tools, evaluation designs, and other resources. Once a number of meetings have occurred, a level of trust will be built that leads to the long-term sustainability of a peer support network around evaluation (as well as other organizational and programmatic challenges) that in most cases lasts longer than the facilitated peer exchange process itself. It is important, especially in the beginning, to have a facilitator for this process who has both evaluation (evaluative learning) and group facilitation skills.

Cost to the funder: medium to high. The financial cost of a peer exchange process is not as high as many funders may think. Consider the following factors with respect to cost: (1) grantees could have to travel a significant distance to spend time with one another, and if so, could have associated costs; and (2) using an experienced evaluator *and* group facilitator to facilitate the process has a benefit and an associated cost. However, when compared to conducting an external evaluation, the cost is less.

Cost to the grantee: medium to high. Grantees' biggest cost is time. For a twelve-month peer exchange group process (not including travel or site visits), participants spend from six to ten days out of the year preparing for and participating in meetings. When funders support site visits, participants are on site for two to four days, and they need to spend time making travel arrangements and preparing for the visits. When participants serve as the host, they have an additional few days preparing for their visitors. Finally, grantee leaders will need to invest a significant number of days if both site visits and group exchange processes are implemented.

Capacity-building potential: high. The participants in the HHMI process all stated that their evaluation knowledge and skills improved, and most important, their peers and the process helped them develop specific strategies and tools for using evaluation efforts to improve their programs and institutions. In fact, the peer exchange process better instilled and institutionalized the evaluative learning approach than developed core evaluation or research skills; however, participants improved and actually implemented and used evaluation skills more than if they had been trained through a workshop.

- **Fund an external evaluator to assess one or more grantmaking programs.** This high-cost strategy won't necessarily improve evaluative learning unless it is implemented in a way that fully engages all of the grantees in an ongoing evaluation process where they have a voice in the entire process, including development of the logic model; evaluation questions, methods, and data collection tools; and what the findings mean.

For example, an evaluation was conducted of the Strategic Solutions Initiative, a jointly funded five-year initiative with the goal of improving the understanding and use of strategic restructuring among funders, consultants, and nonprofit leaders throughout the country. The core strategies included conducting research and sharing what was learned, training consultants on how to facilitate strategic restructuring processes, and disseminating knowledge locally and nationally through workshops and presentations. Evaluation was a part of this initiative from the beginning. The funders—the James Irvine Foundation, the David and Lucile Packard Foundation, and the William and Flora Hewlett Foundation—and the grantee, La Piana Associates, jointly designed the evaluation with the assistance of an outside evaluator. Additionally, these stakeholders all provided leadership with respect to how the data could and should be interpreted.

As a result, when the data showed, for example, that not enough was known about the role that leadership played in a nonprofit's decision to consider strategic restructuring, the initiative's strategies were revised to better address that issue. More specifically, the grantee refocused their research efforts on understanding the role that leadership plays. These changes in strategy would have been less likely if all key stakeholders were not leading the evaluation process. Too often, when one organizational leader oversees the evaluation without other stakeholder leadership and involvement, and that leader doesn't agree with a particular finding, he or she can dismiss it without considering other interpretations or solutions. Having others play a leadership role in interpreting the findings ensures that learning opportunities aren't overlooked.

Cost to the funder: high. External evaluations of grantmaking programs can cost 3 percent to 10 percent of the grantmaking budget. Additionally, funders will have to spend considerable time partnering with the evaluator and communicating with grantees if the process is truly to benefit both the funders' and grantees' learning.

Cost to the grantee: medium. Grantees' most significant cost is time spent preparing for and participating in all evaluation-related planning, design, and data collection, and reacting to findings.

Capacity-building potential: medium. While these evaluative learning-based external evaluations do help build some capacity for the grantees, it is mostly in relation to program development. Most external evaluators do not have the time and experience to provide the kinds of feedback grantees could use to determine which of their strategies achieved the greatest outcome, and in turn which resources were critical to supporting these strategies. This level of feedback, which is not often provided, is really the beginning place for understanding what the evaluation is teaching the grantee regarding improving overall effectiveness. As such, the learning benefits usually stop with a broad understanding of program effectiveness. Additionally, grantees usually understand that the external evaluation will be used to make future grantmaking decisions.

- **Provide funding to grantees to hire their own outside evaluator.** Funders can provide funding for grantees to hire a consultant to conduct an external evaluation of their programs. The cost and capacity-building benefits are similar to those when funders hire an external evaluator, with one key exception: by hiring their own evaluator, grantees can control the design, implementation, and use of the evaluation, which allows them to ask the kinds of evaluation questions that are a priority for their organization. However, if grantees don't understand the value of nor have the knowledge to implement an evaluative learning process, then they likely will still evaluate programs to provide accountability findings to funders and other constituents.

Cost to the funder: high. Funders' cost is primarily funding it provides to grantees to hire an evaluation consultant. A time cost may occur if funders assist in identifying a consultant or if they become involved in the evaluation design.

Cost to the grantee: medium. Grantees will need to spend a considerable amount of time identifying and working closely with an evaluation consultant to design the evaluation. Additionally, an evaluation will take more time if grantees work with the consultant to develop an evaluative learning approach because all organizational stakeholders will need to be directly involved.

Achieving Evaluative Learning When Evaluations Are Conducted "for" the Funder [XV]

How can an organization learn from or find value in an evaluation conducted for a funder? How can an organization gain insight from evaluation data collection when the organization has not designed nor had the opportunity to customize the data collection to meet its information needs? The answer is through collaboration and communication around evaluation.

Funders like the U.S. Department of Education and the National Science Foundation value evaluation results for their own decision making and determination of strategic direction and thus have explicitly defined evaluation requirements, reporting guidelines, and in some instances, prescribed evaluation data collection tools, processes, and protocols. While there is obvious value in these types of structured evaluations for the funders, the value to the organizations often requires further consideration, exploration, and frequently the technical assistance of an outside consultant to manage the evaluation and facilitate its utility.

The following three steps are most fruitful in turning a funder-driven evaluation into a valued input into organizational and program planning, decision making, and the determination of strategic direction.

1. *Structure the organizational planning and management team to include representation of (or input from) an expert evaluator.* Despite the audience for and genesis of the evaluation design (the funder), the organization needs to prioritize and place value in the evaluation. A critical step toward evaluative learning in any environment is the recognition of the evaluation's value and thus, the positioning of evaluation information

Capacity-building potential: variable. If grantees understand the importance of an evaluative learning process and hire a consultant who can support this approach, the capacity-building potential could be high. However, grantees must ensure through the hiring process that the consultant can provide both technical expertise and experience and understands organizational development. If grantees hire an evaluator strictly to conduct an accountability-based external evaluation, the evaluative learning will likely be minimal.

at the organization's critical decision-making levels. If the data and data collection processes are not respected and valued, the likelihood is high that the generated information will be shelved and useless.

2. *Engage an expert evaluator to help the organization consider the application of evaluation findings.* Organizations engaged in the design and implementation of major programmatic efforts rarely have an evaluation expert on staff, let alone someone with the time to sift through the funder-driven evaluation report or data collection processes to identify if, how, and when the data or data collection processes might be applicable to the organization. Thus, an outside evaluation expert is often needed. Funder-driven evaluations may not, on the surface, yield answers to the organization's most pertinent questions; however, informative data can be found—data that can inform decision making and suggest strategic direction at both the programmatic and organizational levels.

3. *Engage the evaluator in expanding the scope of the evaluation beyond the funder-driven activities.* A third consideration for finding value in a funder-driven evaluation environment is an exploration into how the evaluation might be expanded through additional data collection—a tweaking of the evaluation tools, protocols, and processes in such as way as to more fully address the organization's specific information needs. Again, organizations engaged in full program implementation may seek the assistance of an external expert evaluator to assist expanding the project's scope of work around evaluation.

- **Fund the development of an evaluation plan and system for a grantee.** More funders are beginning to fund grantees to hire an evaluation consultant to assist them in designing an evaluation system that they can maintain and utilize even after the consultant leaves. However, these grantees may need some ongoing support as this process is just greatly reduced post-planning and initial implementation. The process of developing an evaluation system can include some or all of the following steps:

  1. Develop a logic model

  2. Develop evaluation questions

  3. Create measures or indicators

  4. Choose data collection methodologies

  5. Write a long-term evaluation plan, including a set of clear evaluative learning goals, objectives, and action steps

  6. Develop data collection tools, including instructions or a manual on how to use the tools

  7. Select data analysis tools and create templates and instructions

  8. Develop, with a technology service provider or in-house technology director, a technology-based system for collecting, analyzing, and reporting on data

  9. Develop report generation tools, including user-friendly means for communicating findings to different constituents

  10. Provide training on managing, maintaining, and using the system, including developing manuals and other training materials

Developing an evaluative learning system allows for evaluation to be institutionalized and therefore to serve in a concrete, ongoing manner. This is an exciting strategy and is in fact most in alignment with the ideal vision of evaluative learning. Some funders and grantees may find that they want to support or implement, respectively, some initial steps in this process, see how it goes, and further develop the system over time.

An example presented earlier to illustrate collaborative design, but also germane to the development of an ongoing evaluation system, is the Massachusetts Cultural Council (MCC). MCC developed an evaluation plan for its START Initiative, a program to provide organizational capacity-building assistance to local cultural councils and arts and cultural organizations throughout the state. This client engaged an outside consultant to serve as a facilitator and to provide evaluation technical assistance, but not to serve as the evaluator. MCC felt it needed expert help with specific methodological issues, but wanted to ensure that the evaluation addressed its ongoing learning needs. MCC asked program staff to participate in a number of consultant-facilitated meetings that laid out the evaluation framework, questions, methods, and measures. Organizational leaders and staff proposed the evaluation questions, methods, and measures; the consultant provided feedback regarding feasibility, and facilitated discussions to ensure that the design addressed their long-term learning goals. As a direct result of this client-led approach, each of the program staff members came away from the process with a clear sense of how the evaluation would meet their specific learning needs and ideas about how they will use the findings to improve their work. Thus, once the system is in place, everyone has a stake in making sure the evaluation occurs in a high-quality fashion.

Developing an evaluative learning system allows for evaluation to be institutionalized. This is an exciting strategy and is in fact most in alignment with the ideal vision of evaluative learning.

As another example, Eureka Communities, a national leadership development program for nonprofit executive directors, is developing an evaluation system that will ensure evaluation findings are always in alignment with organizational decision making. An outside consultant is working on a web-based evaluation system—or dashboard—to provide "real-time" findings in an interactive web-based report that will be current whenever it is needed.

Cost to the funder: initially high, over time medium to low. Initially, funders will need to invest enough money into grantees to do the planning, build the system, and train staff. Technology needs for the system are also a cost. However, costs for the system, planning, and even technology are greatly reduced in subsequent years if the system is built right. It is important to hire a consultant who really understands the evaluative learning approach and can apply organization development services that maximize the long-term learning. The funders' goal should be to support the development of a system that ends up costing grantees less each year than if they were to hire an external evaluator to design and conduct an evaluation.

Cost to the grantee: high. The initial cost, both in terms of money (if grantees have to raise or allocate money beyond what one funder provides) and of time, is high. However, once the system is in place, grantees should have the tools and training they need to significantly reduce the cost after the initial planning and system set up. If the system is designed correctly, grantees should not have to spend more to maintain, refine, and use the system than if they hired an external evaluator.

Capacity-building potential: the highest. This strategy institutionalizes evaluative learning into grantees. This type of system also ensures that grantees have the ability to develop and refine best practice benchmarks in relation to achieving short-term outcomes, and enables them to manage and lead toward improving upon these benchmarks. This is a true sign of evaluative learning that assists grantees in achieving their mission.

Table 2, Evaluative Learning Support Strategies, highlights the various evaluative learning support strategies funders can implement (as presented above), in order from highest to lowest capacity-building potential. The table also presents the feasibility of each strategy for funders of different sizes, funder burden in dollars and time, and organizational (grantee or nonprofit) burden in dollars and time.

Table 3, Feasibility of Evaluative Learning Strategies, page 96, is useful for understanding the feasibility of different evaluative learning strategies for nonprofits of varying sizes, the relative dollar cost to the nonprofit for each strategy, as well as an indication of the potential for ongoing sustainability for the nonprofit (which is key to ensuring ongoing evaluative learning).

Table 2: Evaluative Learning Support Strategies

How funders can work with organizations to make evaluation beneficial for everyone	Feasibility Based on Funder Size			Funder Burden		Organizational Burden		Capacity Building Potential
	Small	Medium	Large	Dollars	Time	Dollars	Time	
Provide an evaluation coach to some or all grantees (page 83)	Maybe	Yes	Yes	Medium	None	None	Medium	High
Sponsor evaluation workshops for some or all grantees (page 82)	Maybe	Yes	Yes	Medium	Medium	Low	Medium	High
Provide professional development for grantees' internal evaluators (page 85)	Maybe	Yes	Yes	Medium to High	None	Low	Medium	High
Provide funding for peer exchange (page 86)	Maybe	Yes	Yes	Medium to High	None	Low	Medium to High	High
Fund the development of an evaluation plan and system for a grantee (page 92)	Maybe	Yes	Yes	High	Medium to Low	High	High	High
Change how evaluation information is requested from grantees (page 80)	Yes	Yes	Yes	None	Medium	None	Medium	Medium to High
Provide funding or referrals to local evaluation providers (page 81)	Yes	Yes	Yes	Medium to Low	Low	None	None	Medium to High
Fund an external evaluator to assess one or more grantmaking programs (page 88)	No	Maybe	Yes	High	High	None	Medium	Medium
Assess the fit between the funder's and grantee's logic models (page 78)	Yes	Yes	Yes	None	Low	None	Low	Medium
Ensure that the funders' mission, vision, goals, and objectives fit with those of grantees (page 77)	Yes	Yes	Yes	None	Low	None	Low	Medium
Align evaluation requirements with what other funders require of the grantees (page 78)	Yes	Yes	Yes	None	Low	None	Low	Medium
Request clear evaluation designs from grantees (page 79)	Yes	Yes	Yes	None	Low	Low	Medium	Low
Provide funding to grantees to hire their own outside evaluator (page 89)	No	Maybe	Yes	High	Low	None	Medium	Variable

Table 3. Feasibility of Evaluative Learning Strategies

How nonprofits can build their evaluative learning capacity	Feasibility Based on Nonprofit Size (Budget)[3]			Cost($)[4]	Ongoing
	Small	Medium	Large		
Hire an internal evaluator	No	No	Maybe	High	High
Hire an external evaluator to conduct an evaluation	No	Maybe	Yes	Medium to High	Low
Provide training for a current staff member to serve as a part-time internal evaluator	No	Maybe	Yes	Medium to High	High
Hire an external evaluator to design an evaluation for the organization to carry out	No	Maybe	Yes	Medium	Medium to High
Hire an evaluation coach	Maybe	Yes	Yes	Medium	Medium
Train all key staff on evaluation and conduct some evaluation activities	Maybe	Yes	Yes	Medium	Medium

[3] Small organization: up to $250,000; Medium organization: from $250,000 to $1,000,000; Large organization: more than $1,000,000

[4] Estimated. Definitive costs depend on the organization's size, program budget, and level of expertise needed to conduct an evaluation.

96

Step 7: Set Criteria,
Select Strategies, and Begin Work

As Step 6 showed, funders can use many strategies to support evaluative learning. To make a choice, funders need to set criteria for allocating resources (by funders and grantees) and how much impact they want to have. Then they can return to Step 6 to select among the strategies listed there. (Appendix D, Select an Evaluative Learning Support Strategy, page 125, is a tool to help funders determine the best strategies given their available resources.) Finally, it will be time to begin work!

Set Criteria

The first task in this step is to set three criteria for determining the best strategy. Typically, three factors influence funders' decision: resources available to funder, resources available to grantee, and the probable impact of an evaluative learning strategy. Let's explore each.

- *Resources available to funders.* As with all activities, available funds and capacity often drive decisions. Funders can provide the following types of resources: grants, staff time, information, and access to other resources such as high-quality evaluation consultants, strong management support organizations, or technical assistance providers. (These latter are usually readily available through the funder's networks and professional relationships with other nonprofit and philanthropic leaders.)

  It is a good idea for funders to determine how many grant dollars they can put toward supporting their grantees' development of evaluative learning processes. There is no rule of thumb, except to say that funders should put as much as they can afford to this important capacity-building tool. Some foundations allocate as much as 5 to 10 percent of their programmatic grantmaking budget toward evaluation.

  In the beginning, the funding will be higher than in subsequent years because of the need to help grantees hire an evaluation consultant or coach, conduct initial design planning, develop the necessary systems (including, perhaps, technology) and tools, and train staff. However, once the systems and capacity are built, the cost to grantees is for any help they may need to revise or update the system, maintain technology and tools, collect and analyze data, and generate presentations of findings. Once institutionalized as a part of staff's job roles and responsibilities and with the necessary tools, even these processes will diminish in cost for both time and money due to ever increasing efficiency. Also, grantees should have resources of their own (staff time, volunteer time, intern time, technology, flexible funds) to contribute. When grantees commit their own resources they are more likely to follow through on implementation, and the use of evaluative learning will more likely become a part of their organizational culture.

Even if funders can't provide funding, they can still support evaluative learning for their grantees through applying other nonmonetary resources, like foundation staff providing direct technical assistance, information on evaluation, and access to other monetary and nonmonetary resources through professional networks, affiliations, and relationships with colleagues. For example, funders may back a management support organization that provides evaluation training workshops or coaching at a greatly subsidized rate or even free. Funders need to make their grantees aware of these opportunities.

- *Resources available to grantee.* Grantees vary considerably as to the money, time, experience, knowledge, and skills they have to conduct evaluation. Through the questions asked of grantees at the beginning of Step 4, funders will have learned a lot about grantees' current evaluation efforts, as well as their readiness for evaluative learning. Funders need to be careful not to ask grantees to conduct evaluative learning processes that are beyond their capacity without some form of additional assistance.

- *The probable impact of an evaluative learning strategy.* The final strategy-shaping consideration is the capacity-building impact of a particular evaluative learning support strategy. There is always a tradeoff between the resource cost of a particular strategy and its capacity-building benefit. Funders need to assess how to maximize the capacity-building gains while taking into consideration their own resources that are available for the effort, as well as their grantees' resources and readiness.

Review these three guidelines—resources available to funders, resources available to grantees, and the probable impact of an evaluative learning strategy. Write a clear statement describing how much of your resources and your grantees' resources will be applied toward evaluative learning, as well as the level of impact you think is viable given the resources you can expend. Refer to Table 2, Evaluative Learning Support Strategies, page 94, and Table 3, Feasibility of Evaluative Learning Strategies, page 95, as needed to help you determine the appropriate expenditure and impact criteria.

Select Strategy

It is time to select a strategy. Appendix D, Select an Evaluative Learning Support Strategy, page 125, contains a useful tool for identifying the best strategy. The evaluative learning strategy that funders select will be determined using all of the information gathered during the preceding steps, as well as the criteria established in this step. More specifically, funders will select a strategy based on the feasibility of each evaluative learning strategy with respect to

- Their desired level of capacity-building impact
- The resources they have to support the evaluative learning process (time, money, and access to assistance)
- The resources their grantees have to support the evaluative learning process (time, money, and access to assistance)
- The requisite level of readiness for funders and grantees
- The requisite amount of evaluation experience grantees need to implement the strategy

At this point funders should have all of this information and be ready to select the most appropriate evaluative learning strategy or strategies. Note that funders may improve their own capacity to support evaluative learning over time and, as such, will become more "ready" to support additional or more effective strategies in the future. Also, their grantees may develop their own evaluative learning capacity and desire to make improvements over time. As such, funders will very likely need to select some short-term, interim, and long-term strategies.

The evaluative learning strategies, as presented, represent a continuum. As funders and nonprofits see their organizations improve through evaluative learning, they will likely desire continued improvement. Funders will need to revisit and perhaps change their criteria (as established during this step) as progress is made. This revisiting of the criteria may lead to funders moving up the continuum of evaluative learning with respect to how much of a capacity-building impact they seek. Over time, they may decide to change the level of resources they wish to apply toward evaluative learning.

Plunge Forward

The steps laid out in this chapter should provide some clear guidance for beginning to develop strategies to support evaluative learning. Not all funders will be able to commit to all of the strategies. Use the steps and tools to assess how best your institution can begin to move toward making evaluation a learning tool that serves your grantees' ongoing plans and decisions and meets your own learning goals.

Summary

Funders can take seven steps to build the evaluative learning capacity of nonprofits:

Step 1: Educate your board and staff. Funders need to tell their boards about the limitations of evaluative learning: outcome data will be more "short-term," use of control or comparison groups will be unlikely, data quality and consistency will still vary, and grantees will need support (financial and technical).

Step 2: Assess organizational readiness. Critical factors that will determine a funder's "readiness" include a history of supporting (or willingness to support) capacity building, a belief that evaluation serves more than just accountability, access to resources to help grantees build their evaluative learning capacity, and patience.

Step 3: Determine where to begin. Funders need to assess their current grant portfolio to select a program or outcome focus for supporting evaluative learning and develop a logic model for the program area of interest.

Step 4: Assess grantees' current efforts. Funders need to talk to their grantees to learn about and assess grantees' current evaluation efforts, and then talk to their grantees' other funders to find out what they require with respect to evaluation and if they would be willing to collaborate to support evaluative learning.

Step 5: Identify a set of grantees to support. Funders then need to assess their grantees' readiness for evaluative learning and decide organizations to invest in.

Step 6: Understand strategies for supporting evaluative learning. To develop a cost-effective evaluative learning support strategy, funders need to determine the amount of resources that both funders and grantees have to invest in the effort, as well as which particular strategy will garner the greatest capacity-building impact.

Step 7: Set criteria, select strategies, and begin work. Funders can choose from and support a number of low-cost to high-cost strategies, with respect to funders' and grantees' time and money.

In the end, this process will serve to make evaluation a win-win process that improves what the entire field knows about best practices, and funders everywhere will be able to make much more efficient and effective use of resources. Now, let the learning begin . . .

A Bright Future

THIS BOOK MAKES A STRONG CASE FOR USING EVALUA-
tion as a capacity-building tool. Specifically, this book presents an
evaluation approach, "evaluative learning," which can effectively
serve to improve nonprofit organizations' programmatic and organizational effectiveness. If the funding community supports nonprofit evaluative
learning, nonprofit organizations will be able to gather information that
improves decisions, inspires others, improves adaptability, increases effectiveness and efficiency, and increases the quality of programs and services.
In turn, these highly effective learning-based organizations, when a part of
a funder's portfolio and given the resources and time to learn, ensure better
use of precious funds for the community's benefit.

Evaluation can also create more opportunities for mutual and fieldwide
learning. By pursuing an evaluative learning approach, nonprofits and
funders together, as part of a learning community, can figure out how to
strengthen programs, better allocate resources, and share successful models. With this shared learning and strategizing comes a much clearer fieldwide understanding of the best practices that serve to achieve the greatest
impact for the people, families, and communities that nonprofits serve.
This, in the end, will make evaluation work for everyone.

To create this kind of change, nonprofits and funders need to change the
way they think about evaluation. They must see that evaluation can be
more than an accountability tool for demonstrating something to someone
else. This book makes the case for shifting toward supporting and using
evaluation in a manner that maximizes the use of what is learned, rather

than serving as the final word as to whether and at what level to continue supporting an organization or program.

Evaluative learning shifts funders and grantees toward designing and implementing a continuous evaluation cycle that examines the whole logic model through a collaborative process, resulting in improved programs and organizations. It can answer the same set of accountability questions as other approaches to evaluation, but it goes much further. Specifically, evaluative learning goes beyond answering the question, Did you achieve your outcomes? and asks, If so, what resources and program qualities were most critical for achieving these outcomes?

If, as a funder, you are only interested in the bottom line (the outcomes), then evaluative learning is likely more than you want. However, if learning about best practices and understanding how organizations can implement them is important, then evaluative learning can be an effective tool.

This book describes a step-by-step process that funders can use to help build the evaluative learning capacity of nonprofits. From this beginning, funders can prepare to use evaluative learning across their grantmaking programs.

If many funders support evaluative learning, where could this lead? Ultimately, the goal is to have many funders supporting many similar nonprofit organizations (nonprofits implementing similar programs and strategies to achieve similar outcome goals) in their efforts to gather, analyze and use data. Specifically, funders would support and nonprofits would lead evaluations that examine and reexamine their entire logic model—the outcomes they achieve, the quality and quantity of programs and services necessary for achieving these outcomes, and the resources needed to deliver the outcomes. With this data and a high level of sharing among these field-specific funders *and* nonprofits, a data-driven process could identify specific research- and practice-based best practices. Nonprofits would play a lead role, with funders and other leaders, in interpreting what is learned. (This has typically been a role that funders only engage researchers and evaluators to play, often absent the nonprofit voice—except as research or evaluation subjects.)

By supporting nonprofits' learning efforts, funders would empower non-profits to lead the development of organizational and programmatic standards of practice—something that, to date, has been difficult for most fields to develop beyond ethical and financial accountability standards. A process of looking across various types and quality of data would be required to assess what truly works. But, in time, widespread use of evaluative learning practices will result in a true understanding of what it takes to succeed.

Look to the sky

Funders often talk about program replicability and standards of practice, but have gone about developing these through traditional research designs that, most would agree, have not delivered generalizable findings. Indeed, many funders might conclude that most nonprofit endeavors are impervious to developing useful standards. But there *is* an example of a fieldwide research effort that could serve as a good model—astronomy. Thousands of independent astronomers, part-timers and hobbyists, collect and share data from their independent observations of the skies. Academic and large-scale institutional astronomers collaborate with these part-timers and hobbyists to share data. The part-time and hobbyist astronomers set their own research agenda and gather the kinds of data that suits their needs (or context), but share the information with others. There are processes, convenings, and meetings (in-person and virtual) where this information is shared. Some of the greatest astronomical discoveries have been made through this collaborative process.

Nonprofits, with support from their funders, can emulate the success of astronomers. Acting as independent researchers to serve their own learning needs, nonprofits can serve to advance their respective fields beyond what a well-funded research study or rigorous evaluation could achieve alone. Of course, this requires that funders invest more in grantees' efforts to evaluate their programs and share their findings. Funders will need to "partner for learning" if this dream is to come to fruition. But it can happen. One need only look to the sky to see that this process has indeed worked very well for others.

Appendix

Note to readers: The following tools can be downloaded at the publisher's web site at the following URL. Simply enter this URL in your web browser and use the following code to download the tools. If you have any difficulties, phone the publisher at 800-274-6024.

http://www.fieldstonealliance.org/worksheets

Code: W482FgE5

These materials are intended for use in the same way as photocopies, but they are in a form that allows you to type in your responses and reformat the material. Please do not download the material unless you or your organization has purchased this book.

Appendix A: Funder Readiness Tool

Instructions: Ideally, funders will engage as many program staff, institutional leaders, and board members as possible in a group process of responding to the following questions. Engaging as many key institutional leaders as possible as this "readiness assessment" process is important as it is also an opportunity to educate decision makers about the value of evaluative learning.

This tool asks funders a series of questions and provides responses that are necessary to fully support grantees' evaluative learning. The shaded response categories are the ideal answers.

If, as your institution answers each of these questions, your answers are not in the shaded response categories, there is "the next step . . ." recommendation that can serve to get your institution ready to support evaluative learning. After completing the questions, you and your institution will want to carefully review the next steps needed to get ready, and develop action steps as suggested or additional strategies to get your institution "ready" for evaluative learning.

Prerequisites: Don't move forward without meeting these first.

1. **Does your institution provide nonprogram funding (e.g., general operating support, capacity-building grants, etc.)?**

   Yes   No

   If no, the next step is to . . . *educate staff and board as to the need for capacity-building and other nonprogrammatic funding*

2. **Does every key institutional decision maker see the value of evaluation beyond accountability?**

   Yes   No

   If no, the next step is to . . . *educate all key decision makers about the long-term benefits of evaluative learning for both funders and grantees*

3. **Can your institution provide access to nonmonetary resources to support grantees (e.g., referrals to technical assistance providers, other funding sources, etc.)?**

   Yes   No

   If no, the next step is to . . . *talk to colleagues, other funders, and community leaders to identify resources that your grantees can access*

4. **Can institutional leaders and decision makers wait two to three years to begin receiving the quality of evaluation findings they need to make decisions?**

   Yes   No

   If no, the next step is to . . . *educate institutional leaders about the time grantees need to institutionalize evaluative learning*

Ideal: Most key institutional decision makers need to be on board.

1. **How many program staff, institutional leaders, and board members believe that evaluation is necessary to determine whether your institution is achieving its mission?**

   All   Most   Fewer than half   None

   If none to fewer than half, the next step is to . . . *educate those who don't see the mission-based value of evaluation or who don't support evaluative learning and provide examples of its value over time*

2. **How often do program staff and institutional leaders (including board members) support or conduct evaluations and use the findings to make decisions?**

   Always   Often   Seldom   Never

   If never to seldom, the next step is to . . . *develop institutional strategies to more effectively integrate evaluation findings into decision making*

Ideal: Most key institutional decision makers need to be on board. (continued)

3. **How often do external evaluation findings get shared with grantees, including allowing grantees the opportunity to discuss the implications of the findings?**

    Always Often   Seldom Never

    If never to seldom, the next step is to . . . *identify and remove the barriers to sharing evaluation findings*

4. **How often do program staff and institutional leaders (including board members) use program evaluation findings to understand and help address their grantee's organizational capacity-building needs?**

    Always Often   Seldom Never

    If never to seldom, the next step is to . . . *develop institutional strategies for using program evaluation findings to inform nonprogrammatic grantmaking decisions*

5. **How often do your institution's current evaluation efforts evaluate the whole logic model (i.e., the inputs, strategies, outputs, outcomes, and "arrows")?**

    Always Often   Seldom Never

    If never to seldom, the next step is to . . . *develop strategies for supporting or conducting evaluations that evaluate the whole logic model, including engaging evaluators expert in using a logic model approach and engaging grantees in logic model development efforts*

6. **How many grantees has your institution supported for three or more years?**

    All Most   Fewer than half None

    If none to fewer than half, the next step is to . . . *determine whether it is possible to support grantees on a long-term basis, and if not, consider supporting capacity-building efforts, like evaluative learning, that will improve grantees' long-term viability and sustainability*

Helpful: Important for funders to have or develop.

1. **How often has your institution's evaluation efforts included the active participation or engagement of grantee organizations?**

    Always Often   Seldom Never

    If never to seldom, the next step is to . . . *begin talking with evaluators and grantees about how to get grantees more involved in evaluation; move forward on getting more grantee participation, when and where possible*

Helpful: Important for funders to have or develop. (continued)

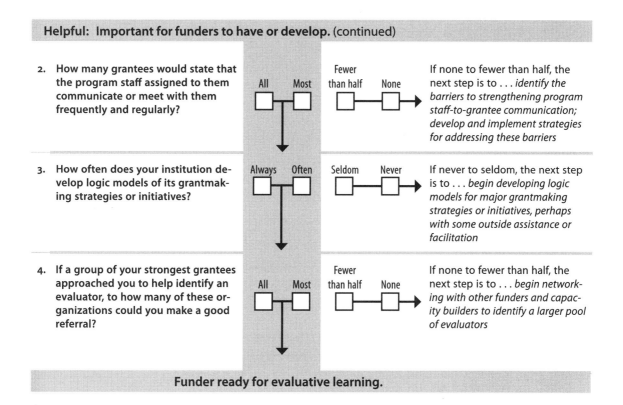

2. How many grantees would state that the program staff assigned to them communicate or meet with them frequently and regularly?

   All   Most   Fewer than half   None

If none to fewer than half, the next step is to . . . *identify the barriers to strengthening program staff-to-grantee communication; develop and implement strategies for addressing these barriers*

3. How often does your institution develop logic models of its grantmaking strategies or initiatives?

   Always   Often   Seldom   Never

If never to seldom, the next step is to . . . *begin developing logic models for major grantmaking strategies or initiatives, perhaps with some outside assistance or facilitation*

4. If a group of your strongest grantees approached you to help identify an evaluator, to how many of these organizations could you make a good referral?

   All   Most   Fewer than half   None

If none to fewer than half, the next step is to . . . *begin networking with other funders and capacity builders to identify a larger pool of evaluators*

Funder ready for evaluative learning.

Appendix B: Logic Model Development Tool

Instructions: Funders and nonprofit organizations can use the following worksheet as a simple tool for developing a logic model. Funders and nonprofits need to identify the key stakeholders they would like involved in developing the logic model. Then, they need to convene these stakeholders and facilitate a process that elicits everyone's assumptions as to their answers to the following questions, ensuring that all individuals fully contribute during the process. Each of these questions needs to be asked and answered fully, in the order that they appear.

1. What is the community-level impact (change) that our organization would like to contribute significantly to creating as a result of our programs?

2. What are the long-term outcomes we would like our clients to achieve? Specifically, what behavioral changes would we like to see our clients make as a result of our programs and services?

3. What are the short-term outcomes we would like our clients to achieve? Specifically, what cognitive, emotional, motivational, skill, or perception change would we like to see our clients make as a direct result of our programs and services?

4. What programs, strategies, or services do we need to achieve the short- and long-term outcomes?

5. What resources or inputs do we need to support strategy or service implementation?

6. What is going on in the community or in our clients' lives that we have no control over but that could affect the quality of our programs or the success of our clients?

Place your responses in the appropriate boxes in the Logic Model Worksheet, and *don't forget to draw arrows* showing the causal relationships between inputs or resources, strategies, and outcomes.

Inputs	Strategies	Outputs	Outcomes	Impact
All of the resources necessary for supporting a program	The specific activities, interventions, services, and/or programs that serve a particular target audience	A short-term measure of program strategy implementation	The short- and longer-term effects of program strategies on client behaviors, attitudes, knowledge, and/or perceptions	The long-term and aggregate effect of a sustained program, service, or intervention on the overall target population.

Environmental Context: Factors beyond our control

Appendix C: Assessing Grantees' Readiness for Evaluative Learning

Instructions: Funders can use this questionnaire to assess their grantees' current evaluation efforts and readiness for evaluative learning. They can ask their grantees to complete the questionnaire by mail, e-mail, or web-based survey. Once funders receive the completed questionnaire, they will have a clearer sense of each grantee's unique evaluation efforts, needs, and readiness for evaluative learning. Additionally, this tool will help funders identify other local funders who are supporting the evaluation efforts of grantees, as well as the types of evaluation efforts these other funders require. Lastly, this tool will help funders identify strong evaluation consultants who can be tapped as a resource for grantees.

Current Evaluation Efforts

1. **Is your organization currently evaluating one or more of its programs?**

   ☐ Yes   ☐ No

   If No, why not? _____

   _____

   _____

   _____

2. **If Yes, rank in order each of the reasons your organization is conducting program evaluations. ("1" represents the most important reason)**

   _____ To report to our funders

   _____ To aid in board functioning or governance

   _____ To aid in fundraising

   _____ To aid organizational or strategic planning

   _____ To share with other nonprofit and community leaders in our area

   _____ To improve our programs and services

   _____ To share with the regional or national field of nonprofits addressing a similar social problem or issue (or providing similar programs or services)

   _____ To aid human resource development

   _____ To make critical decisions on how to use program resources cost effectively

   _____ To get client feedback on the quality of programs and services

   _____ To help gauge whether we are achieving our organizational mission

   _____ Other; please specify _____

   _____

Current Evaluation Efforts (continued)

3. **What, specifically, is your organization evaluating? (check all that apply)**

   ☐ Client outcomes (i.e., changes in client behavior, knowledge, skills, motivation, attitude, or perception)

   ☐ The quality of program delivery (i.e., whether and how core program elements are implemented in relation to guidelines and practices set by the program developers and managers, as well as what is known about "best practices")

   ☐ The quantity of program delivery (i.e., how much service is delivered, how many clients are served)

   ☐ Client satisfaction (i.e., whether clients are satisfied with services)

   ☐ The resources spent on service delivery (i.e., staff time spent on service delivery, money spent on service delivery, or other organizational resources used to deliver services)

   ☐ Other; please specify _____

   _____

4. **What is the design of your evaluation efforts? (check all that apply)**

   ☐ Using control or comparison groups (i.e., comparing clients who have received services with those who have not received services)

   ☐ Using pretest/posttest (or longitudinal) data collection (i.e., gathering client data before and after the intervention to determine the degree of change that occurred)

   ☐ Using posttest-only data collection (i.e., gathering data only after the intervention)

   ☐ Tracking, documenting, or monitoring service delivery (i.e., how much service is delivered, the quality of service delivery, resource use, and client satisfaction)

   ☐ Gathering and analyzing secondary data (e.g., school test performance data)

   ☐ Other; please specify _____

   _____

Current Evaluation Efforts (continued)

5. **What data collection methods does your organization use for its evaluation efforts? (check all that apply)**

☐ Surveys   ☐ Tests of knowledge

☐ Questionnaires   ☐ Interviews

☐ Observation   ☐ Focus groups

☐ Video or other media

☐ Document or materials collection (including histories, drawings, stories, poems, journals, reports, articles, etc.)

☐ Other; please specify _____

6. **Who designs your evaluations? (check one box for each row)**

	Makes design decisions	Contributes to the design process	No role in evaluation design
Board members	☐	☐	☐
Organizational leaders (e.g., executive director, program director)	☐	☐	☐
Program staff	☐	☐	☐
External evaluator (or evaluation consultant)	☐	☐	☐
On-staff evaluator(s)	☐	☐	☐
Administrative staff (e.g., technology manager, financial manager, development staff)	☐	☐	☐
Clients	☐	☐	☐
Community stakeholders or constituents	☐	☐	☐
Funders	☐	☐	☐
Other; please specify	☐	☐	☐

Current Evaluation Efforts (continued)

7. **Who implements the evaluation, including data collection and analysis and report generation? (check one box for each row)**

	Primary evaluation implementer	Provides guidance, assistance, or support to the implementation process	No role in evaluation implementation
Board members	☐	☐	☐
Organizational leaders (e.g., executive director, program director)	☐	☐	☐
Program staff	☐	☐	☐
External evaluator (or evaluation consultant)	☐	☐	☐
On-staff evaluator(s)	☐	☐	☐
Administrative staff (e.g., technology manager, financial manager, development staff)	☐	☐	☐
Clients	☐	☐	☐
Community stakeholders or constituents	☐	☐	☐
Funders	☐	☐	☐
Other; please specify	☐	☐	☐

8. **When was your most recent program evaluation? (check only one)**

   ☐ Never

   ☐ We have **not** conducted an evaluation within the past three years

   ☐ 2–3 years ago

   ☐ 1–2 years ago

   ☐ Within the past year

   ☐ We are conducting an evaluation of programs or services right now

Current Evaluation Efforts (continued)

9. **How often does your organization conduct evaluations of its programs or services? (check only one)**

   ☐ Never

   ☐ When our funders or other organizational stakeholders ask us to

   ☐ Once every 2–3 years

   ☐ Once every year

   ☐ Every six to nine months

   ☐ On an ongoing basis (we are always formally collecting, analyzing, and using program data)

10. **How often do you use program evaluation findings for the following? (check all that apply)**

	Often	Rarely	Never
Program development, planning, and improvement	☐	☐	☐
Organizational planning, including strategic planning	☐	☐	☐
Board or governance decision making	☐	☐	☐
Human resource development and management	☐	☐	☐
Fundraising	☐	☐	☐
Financial management	☐	☐	☐
Marketing	☐	☐	☐
Community outreach (including collaboration, strategic alliances, and networking)	☐	☐	☐
Disseminating information to community constituents	☐	☐	☐
Disseminating information to the field (similar organizations in the region or nation)	☐	☐	☐
Other; please specify	☐	☐	☐

Current Evaluation Efforts (continued)

11. **What percentage of your organization's operating budget is allocated to support your evaluation efforts?**
    _____%

12. **Does your organization receive grants from other funders to specifically support your evaluation efforts?**

    ☐ Yes   ☐ No

    If so, what percentage of your organization's "evaluation" budget do these other funders cover?

    _____%

    Would you share with us who these funders are?

    _____

    _____

    _____

    _____

13. **Please estimate the amount of time the people involved in designing and conducting your evaluation efforts spend per month.**

	Average # of hours per month
Board members	
Organizational leaders (e.g., executive director, program director, etc.)	
Program staff	
External evaluator (or evaluation consultant)	
On-staff evaluator(s)	
Administrative staff (e.g., technology manager, financial manager, development staff)	
Clients	
Community stakeholders or constituents	
Funders	
Other; please specify	

Current Evaluation Efforts (continued)

14. If your organization uses an outside evaluator, how would you rate the evaluator for the following? (Respond for the most recent evaluation consultant that your organization engaged.)

	Poor	Fair	Satisfactory	Good	Excellent	Don't Know
Overall consulting skills	☐	☐	☐	☐	☐	☐
Communication skills	☐	☐	☐	☐	☐	☐
Ability to facilitate group processes	☐	☐	☐	☐	☐	☐
Ability to help synthesize information	☐	☐	☐	☐	☐	☐
Ability to help groups come to consensus	☐	☐	☐	☐	☐	☐
Understanding of organizational development and capacity building	☐	☐	☐	☐	☐	☐
Understanding of logic models	☐	☐	☐	☐	☐	☐
Evaluation design skills	☐	☐	☐	☐	☐	☐
Data collection instrument design skills	☐	☐	☐	☐	☐	☐
Data analysis skills	☐	☐	☐	☐	☐	☐
Ability to present evaluation findings in a way that is most useful to your organization	☐	☐	☐	☐	☐	☐
Ability to educate or train organizational staff on evaluation	☐	☐	☐	☐	☐	☐
Ability to empower your organization's continued use of the evaluation tools and process on an ongoing basis without the consultant's help	☐	☐	☐	☐	☐	☐

15. Would you recommend this consultant to another organization?   ☐ Yes   ☐ No

If so, would you share with us the name of this consultant? _____

_____

Current Evaluation Efforts (continued)

16. From how many of the following types of funders does your organization receive grants?

	Private foundations	Government agencies	Corporations
Total number of funders			
Number of these funders that require your organization to present evaluation findings			

Does your organization have one evaluation process or multiple evaluations going on at the same time?

	Private foundations	Government agencies	Corporations
We have to have a separate evaluation process for each grant	☐	☐	☐
Some of our evaluation processes meet the needs of more than one funder	☐	☐	☐
Our organization has one evaluation process that meets the needs of all of these funders	☐	☐	☐

17. If your organization evaluates its programs, please share with us some of the successful ways in which your organization has made use of the findings.

18. Please share with us some of the challenges your organization has faced in evaluating its programs.

Assessing Organizational Readiness for Evaluative Learning

19. How much do you agree with the following statements?

	Strongly disagree	Disagree	Unsure	Agree	Strongly agree
Organizational leaders support ongoing professional development for staff	☐	☐	☐	☐	☐
Organizational leaders frequently elicit staff input as a part of their decision-making process	☐	☐	☐	☐	☐
Staff are encouraged to participate in organizational planning efforts	☐	☐	☐	☐	☐
Leaders regularly schedule time with staff to share new information pertaining to the organization's work and mission	☐	☐	☐	☐	☐
Leaders regularly schedule meetings to engage staff to share what they're learning	☐	☐	☐	☐	☐
Organizational leaders frequently use program evaluation findings to make decisions	☐	☐	☐	☐	☐
Our board frequently uses program evaluation findings to make decisions	☐	☐	☐	☐	☐

20. Which of the following types of information could your organization immediately share, if asked? And, when was this information produced? (Note: This is a hypothetical question; we're not asking for your organization to include or produce this information.)

	Doesn't exist	2004	2003	2002	2001 (or longer)
Organizational assessment report	☐	☐	☐	☐	☐
Client needs assessment report	☐	☐	☐	☐	☐
Strategic plan	☐	☐	☐	☐	☐
Program evaluation findings report	☐	☐	☐	☐	☐
Documentation of collaborative activity with other nonprofits	☐	☐	☐	☐	☐

Assessing Organizational Readiness for Evaluative Learning (continued)

21. **If your organization has conducted program evaluations, how receptive and cooperative were staff during the process?**

    ☐ Resistant

    ☐ Minimally cooperative

    ☐ Mostly cooperative

    ☐ Very cooperative

    ☐ Fully participated in the process

22. **If your organization has not conducted program evaluations, how receptive and cooperative do you anticipate staff would be during the process?**

    ☐ Resistant

    ☐ Minimally cooperative

    ☐ Mostly cooperative

    ☐ Very cooperative

    ☐ Fully participated in the process

Thank you for your participation! Your answers will help us improve our grantmaking programs. If you have any questions, contact us at _____.

Appendix D: Select an Evaluative Learning Support Strategy

Instructions: Armed with your findings from the Funder Readiness Tool (Appendix A) and Assessing Grantees' Readiness for Evaluative Learning (Appendix C), you will have some sense of your institution's and your grantees' readiness for evaluative learning. The next steps are to judge whether your institution and each grantee is "high," "medium," or "low" with respect to evaluative learning readiness and assess each grantee's evaluation experience. Fill in this information below. With this information and a clear sense of the average size of your institution's typical program grant, you can use the tool on pages 126–127 to assess the feasibility of a set of strategies to support evaluative learning. This tool will also help you understand the potential for each strategy to serve as a capacity-building tool. The goal is to choose a strategy that is both highly feasible and provides the highest possible benefit.

Selecting an Evaluative Learning Support Strategy			
Funder's Readiness Level:	Low	Medium	High
Nonprofit's Readiness Level:	Low	Medium	High
Nonprofit's Evaluation Experience:	Low	Medium	High
Funder's Average Grant Size per Organization: _____			

Selecting an Evaluative Learning Support Strategy (continued)

Feasible	Strategy	Capacity-Building Potential
☐	Provide an evaluation coach to some or all grantees (page 83)	High
☐	Sponsor evaluation workshops for some or all grantees (page 82)	High
☐	Provide professional development for grantees' internal evaluators (page 85)	High
☐	Provide funding for peer exchange (page 86)	High
☐	Fund the development of an evaluation plan and system for a grantee (page 92)	High
☐	Change how evaluation information is requested from grantees (page 80)	Medium to High
☐	Provide funding or referrals to local evaluation providers (page 81)	Medium to High
☐	Fund an external evaluator to assess one or more grantmaking programs (page 88)	Medium
☐	Assess the fit between the funder's and grantee's logic models (page 78)	Medium
☐	Ensure that the funders' mission, vision, goals, and objectives fit with those of grantees (page 77)	Medium
☐	Align evaluation requirements with what other funders require of the grantees (page 78)	Medium
☐	Request clear evaluation designs from grantees (page 79)	Low
☐	Provide funding to grantees to hire their own outside evaluator (page 89)	Variable

[1] Feasibility is based on the assumption that 5% to 10% of grantmaking budgets should be allocated to evaluation;
✓- = feasible for a small group of grantees; ✓ = feasible for many grantees; ✓+ = feasible for all grantees
[2] These are gross approximations that only provide a general sense of cost; costs vary based on daily rates of capacity builders and evaluators, region of the country, availability of capacity-building resources, etc.
[3] Based on a funder's assessment of their readiness using the "Funder Readiness Tool" in Appendix A
[4] Based on an assessment of a nonprofit's readiness using the Questionnaire in Appendix C
[5] Based on an assessment of a nonprofit's readiness using the Questionnaire in Appendix C

Feasibility Based on a Funder's Average Grant Size per Organization[1]						Approximate Cost per Grantee[2]	Funder Readiness Level Needed[3]	Nonprofit Readiness Level Needed[4]	Nonprofit Evaluation Experience Needed[5]
<$5,000	$5,001–$15,000	$15,001–$25,000	$25,001–$50,000	$50,001–$100,000	>$100,000				
		✓–	✓	✓+	✓+	$3,000–$6,000+[6]	Medium to High	Medium	Low to Medium
✓	✓+	✓+	✓+	✓+	✓+	$100–$1,000+	Medium	Low	Low
		✓–	✓	✓	✓+	$1,500–$5,000+[7]	Medium to High	Medium	Low to Medium
✓–	✓	✓	✓	✓+	✓+	$500–$7,000+[8]	Medium to High	High	Medium to High
			✓–	✓	✓+	$10,000–$50,000	Medium	Medium to High	Medium to High
✓+	✓+	✓+	✓+	✓+	✓+	$0	Low	Low	Low to Medium
✓+	✓+	✓+	✓+	✓+	✓+	$100–$7,000+[9]	High	Low to Medium	Low to Medium
			✓–	✓	✓+	$10,000–$75,000+	Low to Medium	Low to Medium	Low
✓–	✓	✓	✓	✓+	✓+	$0–$1,000+[10]	Low to Medium	Medium	Medium
✓+	✓+	✓+	✓+	✓+	✓+	$0	Low	Low	Low
✓+	✓+	✓+	✓+	✓+	✓+	$0	Medium	Low	Medium
✓–	✓	✓	✓	✓+	✓+	$0–$25,000+[11]	Medium to High	High	Medium to High
			✓–	✓	✓+	$10,000–$75,000+	Medium to High	High	Medium to High

[6] Assumes a daily "coaching" rate of $500 to $1,000, and six days of coaching per year

[7] Assumes more in-depth training on evaluation methodology; i.e., beyond the basics

[8] At the low end, covers costs of local or regional travel and related expenses; at the high end, includes long-distance travel and four days of an evaluator's time to provide technical assistance or facilitation

[9] Management support organizations can provide workshops, training, coaching, and consulting to nonprofits in a particular region

[10] Cost depends on a nonprofit's experience developing a logic model and their need for outside assistance

[11] Cost depends on whether a nonprofit needs outside assistance with designing an evaluation system

Notes

i. Michael Q. Patton, *Qualitative Evaluation Methods*, 2nd ed. (Thousand Oaks, CA: Sage Publications, 1990), 129.

ii. http://www.stanford.edu/~davidf/empowermentevaluation.html.

iii. Paul Connolly and Carol Lukas, *Strengthening Nonprofit Performance: A Funder's Guide to Capacity Building* (Saint Paul, MN: Amherst H. Wilder Foundation, 2002).

iv. *Strategic Solutions 2000–2001* Evaluation Report (New York: The Conservation Company, 2001).

v. Paul Connolly and Peter York, *Building the Capacity of Capacity Builders: A Study of Management Support and Field Building Organizations in the Nonprofit Sector* (New York: The Conservation Company, 2003).

vi. Christine Letts, William Ryan, and Allen Grossman introduced the concept of adaptive capacity in *High Performance Nonprofit Organizations: Managing Upstream for Greater Impact* (New York: John Wiley & Son, Inc., 1999). Carl Sussman built on this work in a November 24, 2003, working paper, *Making Change: The Role of Adaptive Capacity in Organizational Effectiveness*, which he developed in partnership with Management Consulting Services with support from the Barr Foundation.

vii. *W. K. Kellogg Foundation Logic Model Development Guide* (Battle Creek, MI: W. K. Kellogg Foundation, 2001).

viii. Patton, *Qualitative Evaluation Methods*.

ix. Paul Light, "Weathering the Storm of Reform: Or, How to Ensure Progress as the Sky Clears," in the Report from 2000 GEN-GEO: *High Performing Organizations: Linking Evaluation & Effectiveness* (Washington, DC: Grantmakers for Effective Organizations, 2000).

x. Patricia Patrizi and Bernard McMullan, *Evaluation in Foundations: The Unrealized Potential* (Battle Creek, MI: W. K. Kellogg Foundation, 1998).

xi. R. D. Sumariwalla and M. E. Taylor, "The Application of Program Evaluation in the Management of the Non-profit Sector: An Exploratory Study," in a paper prepared for the 1991 Spring Research Forum Leadership and Management (Cleveland, OH, 1991).

xii. A. H. Fine, C. E. Thayer, and A. Coghlan, *Program Evaluation Practice in the Nonprofit Sector* (Washington, DC: Innovation Network, 1998).

xiii. *Kellogg Foundation Logic Model Development Guide*.

xiv. Marty Campbell and Charles McClintock, "Shall We Dance? Program Evaluation Meets OD in the Nonprofit Sector," in *OD Practitioner* 34, no. 4 (2002).

xv. Chantell Johnson, "How can nonprofits with small programs and budgets participate and engage in evaluative learning?" in *Learning As We Go: Making Evaluation Work for Everyone* (TCC Group, 2003).

Evaluation Resources

Books

Connolly, P., & Lukas, C. (2002). *Strengthening Nonprofit Performance: A Funder's Guide to Capacity Building.* (Saint Paul, MN: Fieldstone Alliance).

Fetterman, D. M., Kaftarian, S. J., & Eandersman, A. (1996). *Empowerment Evaluation: Knowledge and Tools for Self-Assessment and Accountability.* (Thousand Oaks, CA: Sage Publications).

Gray, S. T., & Associates. (1998). *Evaluation with Power: A New Approach to Organizational Effectiveness, Empowerment and Excellence.* (Washington, DC: Independent Sector).

Kibbe, B. D., et al. (2004). *Funding Effectiveness: Lessons in Building Nonprofit Capacity.* (San Francisco, CA: Jossey-Bass).

Letts, C., Ryan, W., & Grossman, A. (1999). *High Performance Nonprofit Organizations: Managing Upstream for Greater Impact.* (New York: John Wiley & Son, Inc.).

Love, A. J. (1991). *Internal Evaluation: Building Organizations from Within.* (Thousand Oaks, CA: Sage Publications).

Mattessich, P. (2003). *The Manager's Guide to Program Evaluation: Planning, Contracting, and Managing for Results.* (Saint Paul, MN: Fieldstone Alliance).

Patton, M. Q. (1990). *Qualitative Evaluation Methods,* 2nd ed. (Thousand Oaks, CA: Sage Publications).

Patton, M. Q. (1997). *Utilization-Focused Evaluation* 3rd ed. (Thousand Oaks, CA: Sage Publications).

Preskill, H. S., & Torres, R. T. (1999). *Evaluative Inquiry for Learning in Organizations.* (Thousand Oaks, CA: Sage Publications).

Russ-Eft, D., & Preskill, H. (2001). *Evaluation in Organizations: A Systematic Approach to Enhancing Learning, Performance and Change.* (Cambridge, MA: Perseus Publishing).

Senge, P. M. (1990). *The Fifth Discipline: The Art and Practice of the Learning Organization.* (New York: Doubleday).

Sonnichsen, R. C. (1999). *High Impact Evaluation.* (Thousand Oaks, CA: Sage Publications).

Articles and Reports

Backer, T. E. (1999). *Innovation in Context: New Foundation Approaches to Evaluation, Collaboration and Best Practices.* (Encino, CA: Human Interaction Research Institute).

Campbell, M., & McClintock, C. (2002). Shall We Dance?: Program Evaluation Meets OD in the Nonprofit Sector. *OD Practitioner,* 34(4), 3–7.

Cherin, D., & W. Meezan. (1998). Evaluation as a Means of Organizational Learning. *Administration in Social Work,* 22, 1–21.

Connolly, P., & York, P. (2003). *Building the Capacity of Capacity Builders: A Study of Management Support and Field Building Organizations in the Nonprofit Sector.* (New York: The Conservation Company).

Easterling, D. (2000). Outcome Evaluation: Theory, Reality and Possibilities. *Nonprofit and Voluntary Sector Quarterly,* 29, 330–334.

Easterling, D., & Csuti, N. B. (1999). *Using Evaluation to Improve Grant-making: What's Good for the Goose Is Good for the Grantor,* a publication of the Colorado Trust. (Denver, CO).

Fine, A. H., Thayer, C. E., & Coghlan, A. (1998). *Program Evaluation Practice in the Nonprofit Sector.* (Washington, DC: Innovation Network).

GEO-GEN. (2000). *High Performance Organizations: Linking Evaluation and Effectiveness,* in the Report on the GEN-GEO 2000 Conference. (Washington, DC: Grantmakers for Effective Organizations).

Grantmakers in the Arts (1999). *Getting Value from Evaluations,* in Proceedings from the 1999 Conference. (San Francisco, CA).

Hasenfeld, Y. Z., Hill, K., & Weaver, D. (2001). *A Participatory Model for Evaluating Social Programs.* (San Francisco, CA: The James Irvine Foundation).

Hernandez, G., & Visher, M. G. (2001). *Creating a Culture of Inquiry: Changing Methods—and Minds—on the Use of Evaluation in Nonprofit Organizations.* (San Francisco, CA: The James Irvine Foundation).

Patrizi, P., & McMullan, B. (1998). *Evaluation in Foundations: The Unrealized Potential.* (Battle Creek, MI: W. K. Kellogg Foundation).

Stufflebeam, D. L. (1997). *Strategies for Institutionalizing Evaluation: Revisited.* (Kalamazoo, MI: The Evaluation Center).

Sumariwalla, R. D., & Taylor, M. E. (1991). "The Application of Program Evaluation in the Management of the Non-profit Sector: An Exploratory Study," in a paper prepared for the 1991 Spring Research Forum Leadership and Management (Cleveland, OH).

Sussman, C. (2003). Making Change: How to Build Adaptive Capacity. *The Nonprofit Quarterly,* Winter, 19–24.

Torres, R. T., & Preskill, H. (2001). Evaluation and Organizational Learning: Past, Present and Future. *American Journal of Evaluation,* 22(3), 387–395.

York, P. Y. (2003). *Learning as We Go: Making Evaluation Work for Everyone.* (New York: TCC Group).

Other Resources

American Evaluation Association. Information about evaluation practices, methods, and uses through application and exploration of program evaluation, personnel evaluation, and technology. http://www.eval.org.

Getting to Outcomes: Methods and Tools for Planning, Self-Evaluation and Accountability. A manual that works through ten questions that incorporate the basic elements of program planning, implementation, evaluation, and sustainability. http://www.stanford.edu/~davidf/empowermentevaluation.html#GTO.

W. K. Kellogg Foundation Logic Model Development Guide. http://www.wkkf.org/Pubs/Tools/Evaluation/Pub3669.pdf.

The Innovation Network. Web-based tools and resources for evaluation, including a logic model development tool. http://www.innonet.org.

Index

f indicates figure
t indicates table
w indicates worksheet

More results-oriented books from Fieldstone Alliance

Funder's Guides

Community Visions, Community Solutions
Grantmaking for Comprehensive Impact
by Joseph A. Connor and Stephanie Kadel-Taras

Helps foundations, community funds, government agencies, and other grantmakers uncover a community's highest aspiration for itself, and support and sustain strategic efforts to get to workable solutions.

128 pages, softcover   Item # 06930X

A Funder's Guide to Evaluation: Leveraging Evaluation to Improve Nonprofit Effectiveness
by Peter York

More and more funders and nonprofit leaders are shifting away from proving something to someone else, and toward *im*-proving what they do so they can achieve their mission and share how they succeeded with others. This book includes strategies and tools to help grantmakers support and use evaluation as a nonprofit organizational capacity-building tool.

160 pages, softcover   Item # 069482

Strengthening Nonprofit Performance
A Funder's Guide to Capacity Building
by Paul Connolly and Carol Lukas

This practical guide synthesizes the most recent capacity-building practice and research into a collection of strategies, steps, and examples that you can use to get started on or improve funding to strengthen nonprofit organizations.

176 pages, softcover   Item # 069377

Vital Communities

Community Building: What Makes It Work
by Wilder Research Center

Reveals twenty-eight keys to help you build community more effectively. Includes detailed descriptions of each factor, case examples of how they play out, and practical questions to assess your work.

112 pages, softcover   Item # 069121

Community Economic Development Handbook
by Mihailo Temali

A concrete, practical handbook to turning any neighborhood around. It explains how to start a community economic development organization, and then lays out the steps of four proven and powerful strategies for revitalizing inner-city neighborhoods.

288 pages, softcover   Item # 069369

The Wilder Nonprofit Field Guide to Conducting Community Forums
by Carol Lukas and Linda Hoskins

Provides step-by-step instruction to plan and carry out exciting, successful community forums that will educate the public, build consensus, focus action, or influence policy.

128 pages, softcover   Item # 069318

Collaboration

Collaboration Handbook
Creating, Sustaining, and Enjoying the Journey
by Michael Winer and Karen Ray

Shows you how to get a collaboration going, set goals, determine everyone's roles, create an action plan, and evaluate the results. Includes a case study of one collaboration from start to finish, helpful tips on how to avoid pitfalls, and worksheets to keep everyone on track.

192 pages, softcover   Item # 069032

Collaboration: What Makes It Work, 2nd Ed.
by Paul Mattessich, PhD, Marta Murray-Close, BA, and Barbara Monsey, MPH

An in-depth review of current collaboration research. Major findings are summarized, critical conclusions are drawn, and twenty key factors influencing successful collaborations are identified. Includes The Wilder Collaboration Factors Inventory, which groups can use to assess their collaboration.

104 pages, softcover   Item # 069326

For current prices, a catalog, or to order call ☎ 800-274-6024

The Nimble Collaboration
Fine-Tuning Your Collaboration for Lasting Success
by Karen Ray

Shows you ways to make your existing collaboration more responsive, flexible, and productive. Provides three key strategies to help your collaboration respond quickly to changing environments and participants.

136 pages, softcover   *Item # 069288*

Management & Planning

Benchmarking for Nonprofits
How to Measure, Manage, and Improve Performance
by Jason Saul

This book defines a formal, systematic, and reliable way to benchmark—the ongoing process of measuring your organization against leaders. This book covers everything from preparing your organization to measuring performance and implementing best practices.

112 pages, softcover   *Item # 069431*

The Best of the Board Café
Hands-on Solutions for Nonprofit Boards
by Jan Masaoka, CompassPoint Nonprofit Services

Gathers the most requested articles from the e-newsletter, *Board Café*. You'll find a lively menu of ideas, information, opinions, news, and resources to help board members give and get the most out of their board service.

232 pages, softcover   *Item # 069407*

Consulting with Nonprofits: A Practitioner's Guide
by Carol A. Lukas

A step-by-step, comprehensive guide for consultants. Addresses the art of consulting, how to run your business, and much more. Also includes tips and anecdotes from thirty skilled consultants.

240 pages, softcover   *Item # 069172*

The Wilder Nonprofit Field Guide to
Crafting Effective Mission and Vision Statements
by Emil Angelica

Guides you through two six-step processes that result in a mission statement, vision statement, or both. Shows how a clarified mission and vision lead to more effective leadership, decisions, fundraising, and management. Includes tips, sample statements, and worksheets.

88 pages, softcover   *Item # 06927X*

The Wilder Nonprofit Field Guide to
Developing Effective Teams
by Beth Gilbertsen and Vijit Ramchandani

Helps you understand, start, and maintain a team. Provides tools and techniques for writing a mission statement, setting goals, conducting effective meetings, creating ground rules to manage team dynamics, making decisions in teams, creating project plans, and developing team spirit.

80 pages, softcover   *Item # 069202*

The Five Life Stages of Nonprofit Organizations
Where You Are, Where You're Going, and What to Expect When You Get There
by Judith Sharken Simon with J. Terence Donovan

Shows you what's "normal" for each development stage which helps you plan for transitions, stay on track, and avoid unnecessary struggles. Includes The Wilder Nonprofit Life Stage Assessment to plot your organization's progress in seven arenas of organization development.

128 pages, softcover   *Item # 069229*

The Lobbying and Advocacy Handbook for Nonprofit Organizations
Shaping Public Policy at the State and Local Level
by Marcia Avner

The Lobbying and Advocacy Handbook is a planning guide and resource for nonprofit organizations that want to influence issues that matter to them. This book will help you decide whether to lobby and then put plans in place to make it work.

240 pages, softcover   *Item # 069261*

The Manager's Guide to Program Evaluation:
Planning, Contracting, and Managing for Useful Results
by Paul W. Mattessich, Ph.D.

Explains how to plan and manage an evaluation that will help identify your organization's successes, share information with key audiences, and improve services.

96 pages, softcover   *Item # 069385*

The Nonprofit Board Member's Guide to Lobbying and Advocacy
by Marcia Avner

Written specifically for board members, this guide helps organizations increase their impact on policy decisions. It reveals how board members can be involved in planning for and implementing successful lobbying efforts.

96 pages, softcover   *Item # 069393*

For current prices or to order visit us online at 🖥 www.fieldstonealliance.org

The Nonprofit Mergers Workbook
The Leader's Guide to Considering, Negotiating, and Executing a Merger
by David La Piana

A merger can be a daunting and complex process. Save time, money, and untold frustration with this highly practical guide that makes the process manageable and controllable. Includes complete step-by-step guidance from seeking partners to writing the merger agreement, and more.

240 pages, softcover   Item # 069210

The Nonprofit Mergers Workbook Part II
Unifying the Organization after a Merger
by La Piana Associates

Once the merger agreement is signed, the question becomes: How do we make this merger work? *Part II* helps you create a plan to achieve *integration*—bringing together people, programs, processes, and systems from two (or more) organizations into a single, unified whole.

248 pages, includes CD-ROM   Item # 069415

Nonprofit Stewardship
A Better Way to Lead Your Mission-Based Organization
by Peter C. Brinckerhoff

The stewardship model of leadership can help you to keep your organization's mission foremost. It helps you make decisions that are best for the people your organization serves. In other words, stewardship helps you do more good for more people.

272 pages, softcover   Item # 069423

Resolving Conflict in Nonprofit Organizations
The Leader's Guide to Finding Constructive Solutions
by Marion Peters Angelica

Helps you identify conflict, decide whether to intervene, uncover and deal with the true issues, and design and conduct a conflict resolution process.

192 pages, softcover   Item # 069164

Strategic Planning Workbook for Nonprofit Organizations, Revised and Updated
by Bryan Barry

Chart a wise course for your nonprofit's future. This time-tested workbook gives you practical step-by-step guidance, real-life examples, one nonprofit's complete strategic plan, and easy-to-use worksheets.

144 pages, softcover   Item # 069075

Finances

Bookkeeping Basics
What Every Nonprofit Bookkeeper Needs to Know
by Debra L. Ruegg and Lisa M. Venkatrathnam

Complete with step-by-step instructions, a glossary of accounting terms, detailed examples, and handy reproducible forms, this book will enable you to successfully meet the basic bookkeeping requirements of your nonprofit organization—even if you have little or no formal accounting training.

128 pages, softcover   Item # 069296

Coping with Cutbacks:
The Nonprofit Guide to Success When Times Are Tight
by Emil Angelica and Vincent Hyman

Shows you practical ways to involve business, government, and other nonprofits to solve problems together. Also includes 185 cutback strategies you can put to use right away.

128 pages, softcover   Item # 069091

Financial Leadership for Nonprofit Executives
Guiding Your Organization to Long-term Success
by Jeanne Bell Peters and Elizabeth Schaffer

Provides executives with a practical guide to protecting and growing the assets of their organizations and with accomplishing as much mission as possible with those resources.

144 pages, softcover   Item # 06944X

Venture Forth! The Essential Guide to Starting a Moneymaking Business in Your Nonprofit Organization
by Rolfe Larson

The most complete guide on nonprofit business development. Building on the experience of dozens of organizations, this handbook gives you a time-tested approach for finding, testing, and launching a successful nonprofit business venture.

272 pages, softcover   Item # 069245

For current prices, a catalog, or to order call ☎ 800-274-6024

Marketing & Fundraising

The Wilder Nonprofit Field Guide to
Conducting Successful Focus Groups
by Judith Sharken Simon

Shows how to collect valuable information without a lot of money or special expertise. Using this proven technique, you'll get essential opinions and feedback to help you check out your assumptions, do better strategic planning, improve services or products, and more.

80 pages, softcover   *Item # 069199*

Marketing Workbook for Nonprofit Organizations Volume I: Develop the Plan
by Gary J. Stern

Don't just wish for results—get them! Here's how to create a straightforward, usable marketing plan. Includes the six Ps of Marketing, how to use them effectively, a sample marketing plan, tips on using the Internet, and worksheets.

208 pages, softcover   *Item # 069253*

Marketing Workbook for Nonprofit Organizations Volume II: Mobilize People for Marketing Success
by Gary J. Stern

Put together a successful promotional campaign based on the most persuasive tool of all: personal contact. Learn how to mobilize your entire organization, its staff, volunteers, and supporters in a focused, one-to-one marketing campaign. Comes with *Pocket Guide for Marketing Representatives*. In it, your marketing representatives can record key campaign messages and find motivational reminders.

192 pages, softcover   *Item # 069105*

ORDERING INFORMATION

Order by phone, fax, or online

Call toll-free: 800-274-6024
Internationally: 651-556-4509

Fax: 651-556-4517

E-mail: books@fieldstonealliance.org
Online: www.fieldstonealliance.org

Mail: Fieldstone Alliance
Publishing Center
60 Plato Boulevard East, Suite 150
St. Paul, MN 55107

Our NO-RISK guarantee

If you aren't completely satisfied with any book for any reason, simply send it back within 30 days for a full refund.

Pricing and discounts

For current prices and discounts, please visit our web site at www.fieldstonealliance.org or call toll free at 800-274-6024.

Do you have a book idea?

Fieldstone Alliance seeks manuscripts and proposals for books in the fields of nonprofit management and community development. To get a copy of our author guidelines, please call us at 800-274-6024. You can also download them from our web site at www.fieldstonealliance.org.

Visit us online

You'll find information about Fieldstone Alliance and more details on our books, such as table of contents, pricing, discounts, endorsements, and more, at www.fieldstonealliance.org.

Quality assurance

We strive to make sure that all the books we publish are helpful and easy to use. Our major workbooks are tested and critiqued by experts before being published. Their comments help shape the final book and—we trust—make it more useful to you.